Wallace-Homestead

PRICE GUIDE TO

PLASTIC
COLLECTIBLES

LYNDI STEWART McNULTY

3 3113 01189 4849

Published in Radnor, Pennsylvania 19089
by Wallace-Homestead, a division of Chilton Book Company

Library of Congress Catalog Card No. 87-50295
ISBN 0-87069-652-1

Cover and text design by Anthony Jacobson
Manufactured in the United States of America

On the cover:
Vinyl Donald Duck, jointed, real cloth outfit, #3524 revised, Dakin,
mint, **$35-$45.** Addison shortwave radio, Bakelite, cranberry with
butterscotch trim, **$1200.** Crescent-shaped jug with Art Deco lines,
red polystyrene (Burrite), the Burroughs Company, 1940s, **$10.**
unmarked red juicer, **$5.**

1 2 3 4 5 6 7 8 9 0   1 0 9 8 7 6 5 4 3 2

To Betty Stevenson McNulty

Contents

Preface

If you're wondering what the next big collecting trend will be, consider plastics. Plastic is a part of our history that will undoubtedly attract collectors as prices escalate on old favorites like Depression glass and 1940s pottery. Even now, Art Deco dealers and nostalgia fans are gradually adding plastic to their collections. Prices are rising, and some special pieces are already in demand.

Why, then, do so many people look horrified when a collector mentions plastic? Perhaps it is because many consider plastic cheap and tacky; they associate it with food containers and toothbrushes. Yet, for years, insightful collectors have been snapping up significant examples of this segment of Americana. The Smithsonian Institution, the Museum of Modern Art, and the Philadelphia Museum of Art all include plastics in their collections.

The exciting news is that you don't have to go to a museum to find the pieces that collectors would label as desirables; you can go out and discover some great buys for your own collection. After all, this is the beginning of the plastic collector's boom. Plenty of people will still be laughing at the idea of collecting kitchen accessories, for example, while clever collectors are finding a lot of choice items so early on. Remember that oak table that sold for a quarter?

As you begin your search for plastic treasures, just remember that collecting is a personal matter. Some collect for investment, some for nostalgia, some for decorative purposes, and so on. Whatever your purpose in collecting, the bottom line is that you collect because you enjoy it. The *Wallace-Homestead Price Guide to Plastic Collectibles* is intended to help you maintain that enjoyment with this newest area of collection.

Acknowledgments

Special thanks to William Topaz of Wallace-Homestead Book Company for pioneering this kind of price guide—the first ever published on collecting plastic.

Thanks also to Betty Stevenson McNulty of Westminster, Maryland, and to Robert Harrison Wickless, also of Westminster. Betty assisted in collecting plastics and documentation, and helped in typing as well. Robert assisted in photography and manuscript organization.

Finally, a special note of appreciation to friends and dealers who provided plastics to be photographed for this book, and who also provided much heretofore unpublished, firsthand knowledge of the subject. Specifically, I would like to thank the dealers at the Brimfield, Massachusetts, flea markets and at Bellman's Columbia Market in Maryland.

Part One

THE NATURE OF

PLASTIC COLLECTIBLES

*Green and red horse walker, **$18.** Also pictured are painted (mostly red) soldiers, **pair, $22.** From the collection of Audrey Meyer, Sykesville, MD.*

1

Introduction

Plastics. For some, the word conjures up images of relatively modern kitchen goods like Tupperware, or maybe they think of the horde of new children's toys on the market. When they hear of antique plastic, they assume it's a contradiction of terms. How can plastic be antique?

Plastics have been around in synthetic form (like Bakelite) for over 100 years, making them antiques in the true sense of the word. In addition, natural plastics such as those of animal origin—like horn—and those of plant origin—like lacquer—were in use long before any synthetic plastics were ever developed.

Then there are the newly collectible plastics, not quite 100 years old, but still valuable to thousands of collectors. Art Deco plastic objects are at the top of the list, as are Bakelite radios, celluloid Donald Duck toys from the 1930s, and more modern plastic collectibles like vinyl Barbie dolls, plastic trains and cars, hard plastic Aunt Jemima kitchen accessories, and crescent moon pitchers. Advertising collectibles, like the Kool cigarettes' penguin salt and pepper shakers and the Mr. Peanut banks, are already bringing good prices at antiques and collectibles shows. Plastic objects can bring hundreds, and even *thousands*, of dollars. In 1982, for instance, a plastic Cartier watch from the 1930s sold for $4,400, according to Andrea DiNoto's *Art Plastic.*

Radio, Fada Bullet in light butterscotch with dark butterscotch trim, $1200.

Best Buys

Among collectors, this recent wave of interest is gradually generating new respect for plastics. Still, in many cases, people continue to overlook the value of certain plastic collectibles, which means you can find them more easily. The following list will give you a general idea of smart buys you should be able to make right now:

Acrylics
Appliances
Bandalasta ware
Beatl products
Clocks (talking ones)
Dakin toys
Holiday-related items (especially candy
    containers)
Hollywood-related collectibles
Jewelry (1960s)
Kitchenware
Pez candy containers
Salt and pepper shakers
Transistor radios (figural or bright ones
    from the 1950s and 1960s)
Walkers
Russel Wright melamine

Condition

Condition is a major factor in pricing any antique or collectible, and plastic is no exception. Unfortunately, evaluating condition is always subjective, but the following guidelines focus on certain factors of the process that are generally consistent.

MIB (Mint—In Box)

This is like-new condition—even the original box or packaging (if it ever had any) is available. The more recently the object was manufactured, the more important it is to the serious collector that the object be in mint condition.

E (Excellent)

An object in excellent condition looks nearly new: It may have slight finish wear, but other aspects are fine. Also, it may not have its original box.

G (Good)

Good means the object may have a scratch or two, or some other minor defect, but it is usable, and in fact, in good shape overall.

F (Fair)

A *fair* item is in less-than-average condition. It has scratches, dents, perhaps a chip or two, and may even have a missing part.

P (Poor)

This type of object is undesirable to any collector. It is broken, has a major element missing, or has some other significant flaw.

Other Tips on Collecting

As already suggested, collecting plastics operates basically the same as collecting anything else. Color, design, and style are all factors that might initially attract you to an object. These are the same qualities that will interest another collector and cause that person to offer a competitive price for the piece. The rarer the object in question, the higher its price.

So the very early, rare plastics command high prices. Art Deco objects are highly desirable, and as a result, pricey. Objects that are nostalgic, such as Aunt Jemima figurines, or that have excellent design qualities, like geometric ball jugs, are also good choices as investments. Sets of objects, such as red plastic kitchen accessories, attract collectors as well, since it's such a challenge to find all the pieces.

When beginning a collection, consider it as an investment, and always buy the best example of any object you can afford. It might be a difference of only a few dollars at the lower end, or of thousands at the higher. In addition, the value of a fine-quality piece will increase more readily than that of a poorer example.

Above all, buy what you like, even if it's not trendy at the moment. Every collectible has its day. Remember that oak, toys, art pottery, and paper collectibles were all "just junk" not too many years ago. You'll be pleased with the object you bought at a low price when everyone else begins to clamor about it. Besides, whether a red-and-white canister set brightens your kitchen or a cheery yellow radio hums in your den, you'll be able to live with it—and you'll have had fun finding it, too.

2

Plastics Defined

In the realm of collectibles and antiques, Bakelite and Celluloid have already been accepted as items worthy of the "serious" collector's time. But saying that you're collecting *plastic* still seems to elicit a negative response. If all this suggests a trend, collecting plastics will nevertheless become increasingly popular as particular types of plastic become familiar. To help you distinguish them more readily, this chapter presents the terms used to define the physical characteristics of plastics: their general qualities, the qualities of specific types, and the differences in the way they're produced. Types of plastics are listed alphabetically within the natural, semisynthetic, and synthetic categories.

Note that you may be able to use the pin test (see Appendix C) for an object that is particularly difficult to identify. Also note that Appendix B is a list of trademarks and their owners, grouped according to the type of plastic the product is made from; this should also help you classify certain collectibles more easily.

General Qualities

Plastics come in every color, from clear or translucent to bright red. They can be hard as a rock or soft as silk. Plastics may also be liquid or solid. Since many plastics are inexpensive, you encounter them in all aspects of everyday life—everywhere from kitchens to automobiles.

The word *plastic*, which became common in the 1920s, comes from the Greek word *plasticos*, meaning *able to be molded*. A scientific definition of plastics tends to be a bit more extensive than that, distinguishing between thermosetting and thermoplastic materials. *Thermosetting* plastics, such as Bakelite, melamine, and urea-formaldehyde, undergo a chemical reaction when subjected to heat; once such a substance is shaped into an object, it is permanently hardened, and the object is thereafter heat-resistant. *Thermoplastics,* which include acrylic, gutta-percha, and polyethylene, can be reheated and reformed.

Synthetic plastics are made through polymerization. Essentially, this means that simple molecules are chemically combined to make larger molecules that might be compared to chains of the basic structural unit. Natural plastics likewise contain chains (of carbon atoms). Quite an assortment of different plastics results from the variety in these chemical configurations.

Types of Plastics

Natural Plastics

Amber

Amber is a translucent, fossilized tree resin used for making jewelry. Dust particles are often visible in products made with it.

Other problems with amber include brittleness and a tendency to wear away. Check the holes of plastic beads for signs of wear; amber ones will show more than synthetics.

Bois Durci

Between 1855 and 1880, a little-known early plastic, bois durci, was made from sawdust and blood or egg albumen. It was heated and molded into objects such as jewelry, knife handles, and dominos, although its primary use was for molded furniture plaques of famous personalities.

Gutta-Percha

Gutta-percha is a relatively rare, rubberlike substance obtained from tropical Malaysian Palaquium trees. The English traveler, John Tradescant, brought gutta-percha back from his travels in the mid-1600s. It was used to make a variety of objects such as the match safe in Chapter 13. Gutta-percha products tend to break easily, making them an even rarer find nowadays.

Horn

For centuries, horn was used to create objects necessary for daily living. It could be cut to make rings and napkin rings, and heated and pressed into spoons. In early America, it was used as a substitute for glass: Light-colored horn could be heated, flattened, and scraped to make a translucent sheet. Occasionally, it was reduced to a jellylike substance and molded. As you might guess, its most popular use was for powder horns, which were often heated and flattened so that they lay flat against the wearer's side. Many of these were decorated with scrimshaw, increasing their value to collectors.

This natural plastic has also served some decorative purpose. Around the turn of the eighteenth century, hair combs sawed from pieces of horn were popular.

Today, all horn objects are collectible and scarce. Look for a yellowish-brown translucent material and signs of age such as scratches and wear marks.

Lacquer

Lacquer is a resin obtained from lacquer trees.

The Chinese first used liquid lacquer by brushing many coats of it onto objects and carving designs into the lacquered surface; these objects bring high prices today.

Boxes, jardinières, and plaques (often bright red) are just a few lacquer products you might encounter in your collecting.

Papier-mâché

Papier-mâché is a molding substance made from a mixture of paper and glue. Objects made from papier-mâché look heavier than they really are. During the nineteenth century, it was popular for everything from furniture to dresser trays. Sometimes it was gilded, inlaid with mother-of-pearl, or japanned.

Shellac

Various cultures have been using shellac, a plastic derived from lac (which is secreted by an insect), for over 2000 years.

Samuel Peck patented a process by which shellac could be made a molding material by the addition of fillers such as sawdust. In this form, its most popular application was for shiny black photograph cases, called union cases, made for daguerreotypes and ambrotypes. Other uses for this substance, which shares gutta-percha's problems of being both hard to acquire and—in its final form—easy to break, include vanity objects and records.

Tortoiseshell

Tortoiseshell objects, made from the shell of the hawksbill turtle, are also prized by collectors today. During the nineteenth century, tortoiseshell was useful in producing items such as small boxes and toilet articles because it could be heated and molded into various shapes.

Look for irregular brown-spotted objects; these may be antique tortoiseshell. Imitations have more of a repeating, swirling pattern.

Semisynthetics

Semisynthetics are made by modifying the chemical composition of a natural material.

Casein

A 1900s product, casein was made from formaldehyde and milk. It is a thermosetting plastic that will soften in hot water.

Available in many opaque colors, casein was often used in early pens. Because it takes a high polish, it is still used for buckles and buttons. Some early buttons are marked *casein* on the back.

Galalith is a tradename you will often hear in connection with casein.

Celluloid (Cellulose Nitrate)

In 1870, an American printer named John W. Hyatt patented his formula for Celluloid. It was the addition of camphor to cellulose nitrate that made his formula different from earlier substances and a significant advance in the production of plastics. Hyatt formed the Celluloid Manufacturing Company, and Celluloid became the first successfully manufactured semisynthetic plastic.

According to Andrea DiNoto's *Art Plastic*, the so-called *Celluloid Era* (dating from the 1880s to the 1920s) produced an amazing 40,000 tons of this plastic. It was used to make vanity sets, combs, straight razors, dolls, toys, carriage curtains, film, collars, dentures, clock cases, jewelry, and shoe horns, and these are but a few of its many applications.

Celluloid, a thermoplastic which often appears very thin, was tremendously suc-

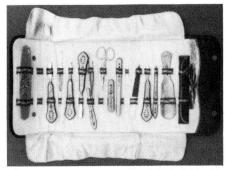

Manicure set, green pearlized Celluloid with black trim and folding travel case, 15 pieces, $40.

cessful because it could be processed in so many ways: buffed, polished, carved, sawed, blow-molded, turned, planed, and stamped from sheets. In addition, it would resist oil, water, and diluted acids, and it cost less to produce than the natural materials it imitated.

Unfortunately, Celluloid had many bad qualities as well. It cracked, dented, and split. Its greatest failure was that it was highly flammable, causing it to be eventually replaced by other plastics. (Remember this as you store your Celluloid, keeping it away from heat, flame, and sunlight.) It is still manufactured today, but most collectible objects were manufactured before the 1950s.

Celluloid was available in over 200 colors, although in collecting, you will see mostly pastels and the well-known color made to resemble ivory. In this book, the word *cream* denotes the lighter ecru colors, and ivory denotes those that have yellowed like real ivory. (In fact, you will see striations in some Celluloid similar to those on real ivory. The ones on Celluloid, however, are more evenly spaced and closer together.) Look for the word *ivory* in many tradenames for Celluloid products.

Pearlizing Celluloid (and later, other types of plastic) products created an interesting color variation that you'll see in a number of collectibles. The pearlizing pro-

17

cess involved mixing guanine (fish scales) with man-made resins to make a substance called *pearlessence*. Pearlized plastics were made with the iridescent look of mother-of-pearl, but often in base colors such as red instead of in the more realistic white or gray.

Although Celluloid was Hyatt's trade name for his product, it is now used by collectors to denote all cellulose nitrate collectibles, many of which are true antiques. Pyralin and Pyroxylin are two other tradenames you will commonly hear in reference to Celluloid objects, especially pens.

Cellulose Acetate
In 1900, a Frenchman named Henry Dreyfuss invented a less flammable thermoplastic substitute for Celluloid called *cellulose acetate*. By the 1920s, cellulose acetate was widely used, especially in what was then the recently developed injection molding process.

This thick (and often, glossy) plastic was popular in the manufacture of jewelry. In fact, Berkander's brightly colored jewelry (see Chapter 19) is made of cellulose acetate. These days, toothbrush handles and eyeglass frames are often made from it.

Cellulose acetate is hard for collectors to distinguish from cellulose nitrate, so both go by the name *Celluloid* in current collector markets. One distinctive quality of this substance, however, is that it resists all solvents except keytone, but absorbs water and becomes distorted.

Ebonite
Since ebonite was the first semisynthetic material, its manufacture was a milestone in plastics history. Little is known about its early history, since its actual application was not exploited until years later.

This black, molded plastic has the faint odor of sulfur. Over the years it acquires a yellowish cast.

During the nineteenth century, ebonite was a popular replacement for jet in jewelry and other small objects. Now, ebonite items are *very* rare finds.

Parkesine
In *Plastics: Common Objects, Classic Designs*, Sylvia Katz writes that Parkesine moldings are considered the oldest objects created from a man-made substance. Although a Swiss alchemist developed the first formula for Parkesine in the 1840s, an Englishman named Alexander Parkes was the first to add camphor to it. In the mid-1800s, Parkes' factory molded this substance into a wide variety of objects including buttons, combs, handles, box lids, plaques, and even letterpresses. These products were often inlaid with expensive materials or pigments added for a marbleized effect.

After Parkes gave up the business, Daniel Spill continued (for approximately 25 years) to manufacture objects under the names Xylonite and Ivoride.

Since it is quite brittle, Parkesine breaks easily. As a result, Parkesine moldings are rare and command high prices.

Vulcanized Rubber
Vulcanized rubber, another antique plastic, was patented by Thomas Handcock in England in 1843. A year later, Charles Goodyear patented vulcanized rubber in America.

Often used to make molded objects, this semisynthetic is vulcanized to make it elastic. When the process is carried to extremes, the rubber becomes hard.

Like ebonite, vulcanized rubber has a sulphuric smell and acquires a yellowish cast as it ages. Articles made with it should not be exposed to heat.

Synthetics
These are either man-made plastics or fully synthetic resins.

Acrylic

Acrylic, a lightweight, petrochemical plastic, was first developed in 1927. Most people probably identify this plastic by the DuPont tradename *Lucite* or by the Rohm and Haas Company tradename *Plexiglass.*

Acrylic is most valued for its transparent and translucent qualities (see "Robert the Robot" in the color section). You'll often see it used as a glass substitute when safety or weight factors are important considerations.

Acrylic's worst quality is that it is easily scratched. Another drawback is its lack of resistance to heat, and older acrylics tend to yellow as well.

A highly versatile plastic, acrylic can be cut, shaped, drilled, extruded, cast, or molded into sheets, rods, or tubes. It can be given a glossy or dull finish, and its surface can be etched, carved, painted, or sandblasted. You will even see faceted acrylic jewelry from the 1940s. Another popular form from the 1940s (and 1950s) was heat-twisted acrylic, seen in the lamp pictured in Chapter 8.

Sometimes acrylics are confused with other transparent plastics. A pin test (see Appendix C) produces a fruity smell. In its normal state, however, an acrylic has no smell or taste.

Bakelite (Molded Phenolic)

Bakelite, the first *entirely* man-made plastic, was the real beginning of the modern plastic industry. In 1907, Dr. Leo Baekeland took out the first of his 119 patents related to the discovery of Bakelite, and, in 1910, he formed the General Bakelite Company. *Bakelite* is really a brand name of a plastic also called phenolic, phenolic resin, or phenol-formaldehyde, but the name has been so heavily used for all objects made of this substance that it has become generic as well. This is due, in part, to the similarity in formula of phenolic resins, but

Wine Art Deco necklace, Bakelite, $95. Wine oval medallion with back-carved flowers, poured resin, $90.

also to the fact that plastics are often hard to identify. (See "Catalin," below.)

Bakelite is a molded phenolic with many characteristics that made it desirable to manufacturers. A heat-resistant (thermosetting) plastic, it was a good choice for radio and appliance cabinets, iron handles, and electrical parts. In addition, Bakelite was resistant to moisture, abrasion, and acids and alkalis. Fillers made it even better. Asbestos, for instance, made it more resistant to heat.

On the other hand, Bakelite could not be produced in white or pastel colors because its resin was amber. Specifically, it is most often found in browns and blacks because of the color restraints of its formula and its preparation method. (You may, however, see it painted white.) It is sometimes found in other colors like burgundy, scarlet, blackish green, blackish blue, and marbled (or even spotted) colors. On rare occasions, you will see transparent molded phenolics.

Also to its disadvantage, Bakelite turns darker or fades with age, yellows when left outdoors, and can turn dull and brittle. The fillers used in it may expand when exposed to water. You will often find cracked pieces of Bakelite which have little gloss left.

Catalin (Cast Phenolic)

Although, as mentioned above, all phenolics tend to get called Bakelite, radio collectors identify cast phenolics by the brand name *Catalin* because of the large number of radio cabinets made from that particular resin.

Catalin, a rather thick plastic, possesses a translucent quality. It offers a wider range of colors than do molded phenolics, including bright color combinations and two-tone marbling effects. However, it does tend to fade with exposure to light, and it is not as heat-resistant as the molded resin, Bakelite.

By the 1950s, Catalin had become too expensive to use.

Most phenolics have an odd identifying odor that you can smell without performing a pin test.

Note: You should be aware that, because of collecting's blurred distinction between cast and molded phenolics, most of the phenolics listed in this book have been identified by collectors using the trade name *Bakelite*, even if they are cast phenolic. This is similar to the situation involving the trade name *Celluloid*, which is now generically used to describe any cellulose nitrate objects (as mentioned above).

Ethenoid Plastics

This group of petrochemical plastics is made up of ethylene derivatives.

Polyethylene (PE). Polyethylene was developed in 1933, but it was not popularly used for household products until after World War II. This thermoplastic has a waxy feel and is best known for its use in Tupperware, first produced in 1945. Another well-known trade name for polyethylene is DuPont's *Polythene*.

Polyethylene is made in both hard and soft forms. Other flexible (but tough) polyethylene products include toys, squeeze bottles, and even artificial flowers. In its harder state it is best known for brightly colored objects, especially housewares and toys.

Polyethylene is still tremendously popular because it can be transparent or colored; it resists liquids, scratches, and organic solvents (below 120°F); and it's tough and nontoxic. An added benefit is that polyethylene will float.

Polypropylene (PP). Another very popular ethenoid is polypropylene, the lightest and least expensive common plastic. This thermoplastic resists chemicals, boiling water, and scratches. It is waxy—especially the flexible variety—and will float if it does not have heavy fillers. Polypropylene can also be molded with a glossy finish. Its most unique application is a molded-in hinge often used to attach lids to containers.

Polypropylene is often used with injection and blow-molding techniques. Collectible objects were made from this plastic after WWII and include both flexible and hard types of polypropylene (baby bottles, housewares, furniture, appliance parts, and luggage, for instance).

Polystyrene. The manufacture of polystyrene, another thermoplastic, became significant during the 1930s. In the 1960s, rubber latex was added to give it better impact-resistance.

Polystyrene is an inexpensive hard plastic that has a metallic feel. When you tap it, you hear a metallic sound. While polystyrene is often made in bright colors, it can also be transparent. It is acid-resistant, easily molded, and resists attack by strong alkalis, strong mineral acids, and many solvents. It does not absorb water and is a good electrical insulator.

On the other hand, it softens at temperatures below the boiling point (about 150°F), is attacked by gasoline and some other hydrocarbons, and is sensitive to some solvent actions. It has poor ultraviolet light resistance and is also brittle.

The most collectible objects in this category are kitchenware items, but polystyrene is also used for disposable tableware, housings for electrical appliances, toys, jewelry, radio cabinets, novelties, bottles, and other household articles.

Vinyl. Vinyl comes in a wide range of both hard and soft plastics. It is an inexpensive, tough thermoplastic that softens only at high temperatures. Vinyls resist chemicals, hot organic solvents, and abrasion. They can be made in any color and may be transparent or opaque as well.

One of the most commonly known types of vinyl is polyvinyl chloride (known in the industry simply as PVC), widely used because of its flame resistance. Production of PVC began in the 1920s and was expanded in the 1930s. It is often prepared as sheets, extruded, molded, and calendered.

The most common vinyl products are toys, dolls, records, and imitation leather.

Fiberglass

This is a fiber-reinforced plastic often used for planters and larger household objects such as furniture, cases, and housings. It has also been valuable to the automotive industry in the production and repair of bodies for cars.

Foamed Plastics

These plastics are formed when gas bubbles are blown into liquid plastic. They are very light, and have little strength. Such plastics are common and inexpensive today.

Vinyl Dakin mouse toy (name unknown) wearing a vinyl top hat and a velvety, red cloth jacket, $28.

Melamine

Melamine-formaldehyde, simply called *melamine*, was developed by the American Cyanamid Company in 1937. A thermosetting amino-plastic, melamine is better than its predecessors, the urea plastics, because it is harder, stronger, and more moisture-resistant. It is also heat- and acid-resistant, is easily colored, and will not yellow. In addition, it can be steam-sterilized and has a glossy, dust-free surface. All of these properties make it useful as dinnerware. (Melamine was also used in lamp shades and buttons.)

The most collectible pieces in this category are streamlined shapes like Russel Wright's Residential pattern, winner of the Museum of Modern Art's Good Design Award for 1953 and 1954. Collectors have just discovered Wright's work, so snap this melamine up while you can. (See Chapter 6 for more information.)

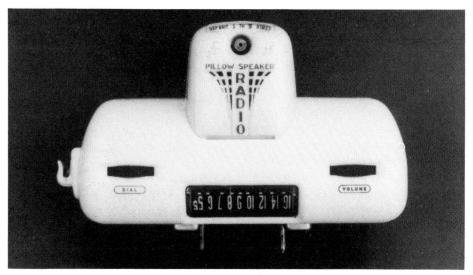

Pink 1950s Pillow Speaker radio, urea, marked DEPOSIT 1 TO 5 DIMES, *the Dahlber Co., Minneapolis, $175. It was originally used on the headboard of a motel bed.*

Keep in mind that although melamine is marketed as scratch-resistant, it will scratch. Try for pieces in unmarred condition.

Urea Plastics (Amino-Plastics)

In an effort to provide the public a wider range of colors not available in Bakelite, the British Cyanides Company developed a thermosetting amino-plastic called urea thiourea formaldehyde in 1924. (It was manufactured under a wide variety of tradenames, like most plastics, including those already discussed in this chapter.) In 1929, the American Cyanamid Company was licensed to produce urea as well.

Urea was the first transparent resin, making it easier to color. With fillers added to give it strength, and a wide range of attractive, marbled colors offered, this was another plastic well-suited to dinnerware. As Andrea DiNoto points out in *Art Plastic*, white urea became popular for the hygiene look of personal appliances such as razors. Other products produced in urea were buttons, tabletops, and lampshades.

Eventually, urea thiourea formaldehyde was improved by a better urea-formaldehyde substance (in 1932). Bright and pastel colors supplanted the marbleized colors favored earlier.

Urea is still manufactured today, although it is now primarily used for closures, appliance housings, and kitchen and bath details.

While urea products are heat- and alkali-resistant and nonyellowing, they are susceptible, unfortunately, to cracking, warping, and brittleness. They swell slightly in water and are not acid-resistant.

Production Methods

Use the following categories—which describe how plastic objects are formed—to identify your collectibles more precisely.

Blow Molding

Blow molding produces hollow objects by forcing hot air into a plastic tube until the plastic expands and forms the shape of the surrounding mold.

Calendering

In this process, rollers spread liquid plastic over another substance; it's a bit like spreading peanut butter on bread.

Casting

As with plaster, casting plastic simply involves pouring the plastic into a mold of the desired shape.

Compression Molding

This molding technique operates rather the same as using a waffle iron. Heat and pressure are applied to a molding compound placed in a heated clam-shell mold. This forces the compound to flow around the shape of the mold.

Look for a flow-mark imperfection on the surface of these objects. You can often find a seam on compression-molded items such as melamine plates.

Extrusion

Extrusion produces tubes and filaments by forcing softened plastic through a tube-shaped die.

Injection Molding

In the high-speed process of injection molding, heated plastic granules are forced into a cold mold.

Laminating

An object is laminated when it passes through a pair of rollers which coat it with melted plastic, forming a sort of sealed-off sandwich around the item.

3
Predominant Styles

Recognizing the style associated with a particular time period is another asset to wise collectors. Not only does the style give clues as to the age and value of a piece; it also gives you an idea of any cultural significance the piece may have. That kind of significance, remember, might account more for your personal interest in a collectible than any other factor.

Early Plastics

The older plastic collectibles usually originated as imitations of more valuable objects characteristic of the Victorian (late 1800s) and Edwardian (turn-of-the-century) styles of the respective time periods. These early plastic objects, then, tended to be quite elaborate and ornate, and were produced to copy natural materials such as ivory and semiprecious stones.

Not many examples of such early plastics exist, compared to those available from the 1930s and later.

Art Nouveau

Also around the turn of the century, the Art Nouveau style produced a number of Celluloid objects characterized by flowing lines, vines, and women with long, flowing hair. There are only a few of these objects left today, and they are expensive. Keep a close watch for them.

Art Deco

Many of the popular collectibles pictured in this book represent the Art Deco trend of the 1920s and 1930s. This style was first introduced in Paris at the *Exposition Internationale des Arts Décoratifs et Industriels Modernes* in 1925, but the term *Art Deco* was not coined until years later.

Quality Art Deco pieces feature careful handwork, good construction, and superior design. Signed pieces are almost always worth more.

Features

The *Deco* style, as many collectors now refer to it, was marked by all of the following recurring themes.

Chrome
Chrome, frequently used in combination with plastics (mostly Bakelite), became a symbol of modern times. Notice the chrome-accented cigarette box in Chapter 13.

Cubism
Cubism, a movement popularized by artists such as Picasso and Braque, also contributed to the Deco style. Squares, circles, rectangles, and triangles began to appear everywhere.

Dandy/Flapper

You'll find the 1920s Flapper and her side-kick, the top-hatted Dandy in his tuxedo, on many plastic items from this period. The couple might even have a *borzoi*, a large, slender, long-haired dog indicative of wealth in their society.

King Tut's Tomb

The opening of King Tut's Tomb in 1922 influenced many designers and created a fascination with Egypt. As a result, Egyptian motifs appeared everywhere.

Dorics, introduced in 1931, are an example of the Egyptian influence on Art Deco. These new, 12-sided pens came in colors intended to evoke the exotic Far East: Kashmir Green, Burma (pearlized dark gray), Cathay Green (pearlized-green-lined), Jet Black, and Morocco (burgundy).

Speed

The 1920s and 1930s became the Machine Age as speed grew to be a major concern. Automobiles were all the rage and airplanes were a constant source of dinner talk. Thus you'll find arrow lines, airplanes, cars, and racing dogs such as whippets incorporated into the design of many plastic Art Deco objects. Streamlining, highly important to speed, became a popular design concept, even carried over in such things as Eversharp Skyline pens.

Dating Your Art Deco Collectibles

The characteristics listed below will help you determine an approximate date for many Deco items.

Early (1910–1935) Art Deco suggests a smooth transition from the curvilinear Art Nouveau:

- Graceful lines
- Deer
- Doves
- Nudes

Pierced blue, fountain-shaped napkin holder, Hommer Manufacturing Co., $8.

- Garlands
- Baskets of flowers
- Jets of water
- Fountains

Later Art Deco objects adopted the more severe or commercialized, mass-produced forms that had become popular, marked by

- Cubism
- Straight lines
- Stark simplicity
- Austerity
- Chrome
- Steel tubing

Many of these later objects also feature mother-of-pearl inlay.

The 1940s

Even though the 1940s were lean years, natural materials were so scarce that plastics research actually increased. You'll find an interesting variety of collectibles from this period.

Dime Store Days, by Lester Glasner and Brownie Harris, recalls the five-and-tens that thrived in the forties. During the war years, many patriotic, red-white-and-blue items were produced, such as the rhinestone and Bakelite USA pin (now valued at $65–$85) shown in *Dime Store Days.* I've included some Bakelite "V for Victory" pins in Chapter 19 because they seem to convey the same patriotic spirit, even though they're not in the traditional colors.

Airplanes were on everyone's mind, too, so you will notice many airplane and propeller motifs in plastic collectibles made during these years. Don't forget the war toys, either: There are plenty of plastic Disney and Christmas items still available to collectors.

These were also the years of Carmen Miranda, "The South American Bombshell" who wore stacks of jewelry, mostly in the shape of fruits such as Bakelite cherries and bananas. You can see these very expensive items pictured in Chapter 19.

Assorted other items from this period do well on the collector's market. Look for bomb-shaped Bakelite salt and pepper shakers for $30, or in other types of plastics for $12. Certain ethnic items from the 1940s—a "Mammy Memo" for example, which would sell for $65 in good condition—are attaining unbelievable prices. Colorful 1940s novelty radios, like the painted Bakelite Charlie McCarthy Majestic, are also selling high ($1000, in this instance). And don't overlook engraved and heat-twisted acrylics from this period, which are often mistaken for much later objects. Finally, keep track of Hollywood-related items, which should do especially well following the one-hundredth anniversary of the "Motion Picture Capital."

The *Populuxe* Era

In his book *Populuxe*, Thomas Hine describes the trends of the period from 1955 to 1965. Calling it "a time that truly believed in the future," he also describes it as a time of keeping up with the Joneses and giving Tupperware parties. Since there was so much industrial expansion, there were plenty of jobs around that paid well, and the generation that had been deprived of luxuries during World War II now wanted to indulge in them.

*Photograph holders made of heat-shaped acrylic with glass inserts, **each, $15.***

In this age of materialism, considering the initial rush to purchase goods after the war was over, manufacturers began to promote *planned obsolescence.* That is, a new product would soon become obsolete as a different model, style, or color replaced it the next year. Hines describes it as a "disposable world." Referring to the manufacturers, he says, "They wanted their new customers to be pleased with their existing products, but not so contented that they would not be tempted to replace them when the new, improved model, with many new and exciting features, was introduced." (In fact, the model often looked different, but was really just an earlier model in disguise.)

Plastics thrived in this era, which produced a lot of collectibles that you might recognize.

Boomerang and Parabola

The bommerang and parabola were often-used shapes of this era. Right after World War II, South Pacific themes were popular (see Chapter 19), and this contributed to the eventual popularity of the boomerang shape. In addition, boomerangs had a mystical connotation because they always returned to the thrower.

Symbolic of speed and of the future, the boomerang was sometimes visually interpreted as airplane wings tilted backward. Even the artist's palette could be seen as a form of the boomerang.

27

Airplanes

Styles of everything from kitchenware to appliances were influenced by the shapes of airplanes. Pre-1950 airplanes had a streamlined look, but more rounded shapes, while post-1950 airplanes had more angular shapes. The newer delta-wing shapes, which were basically short triangles, were used in all kinds of plastic designs during the 1950s. (See the brown bed lamp with the metal reflector in Chapter 8.)

Tailfin

The tailfin, first used on the 1948 Cadillac, became symbolic of luxury during the 1950s. The idea of adding a tailfin to a car was first conceived by Harley Earl, a Hollywood car customizer. Earl said the idea was inspired by the P-38 airplane, and the then-current fascination with airplanes may well have contributed to the popularity of the tailfin. At any rate, you see this form translated to many plastic products.

Color

As part of the planned obsolescence idea, colors were changed often and advertised as "this year's" colors. Most of them seemed unnatural or manufactured.

Look for two-tone items from this period to be highly collectible. Even plastic radios, which were advertised as having "sports car styling," were two-tone: pink and charcoal or turquoise and black.

Sensitive line

The sensitive line was a concept borrowed from the works of artist Paul Klee. Common interpretations include objects made with thin wire structures holding up a heavier-looking form. Ashtrays, kitchenware, and even plastic clocks adopted this style.

Such objects are already becoming some of the most desirable of the time. For examples, look at the flying-saucer lamp (facing page) and the lamp with the three-legged base (near the beginning of Chapter 8).

The Blob and the Artist's Palette

The blob was a motif that had appeared in other art forms much earlier, but did not become popular until the 1950s. Amoeba-like abstract shapes can be found in objects ranging from plastic ashtrays to the blonde, Formica-topped coffee tables of the 1950s ($50–$125 each).

The artist's palette became a popular theme in plastics partly because of this (and partly because of the fascination with the boomerang shape, mentioned earlier). Plastic serving pieces ($10–$20) incorporate this shape into their design.

The Atom

The Atomic Age is another common name for this era, and it is not surprising to find atomlike forms in all varieties of household objects. You might, for instance, find a clock or lamp made to resemble one of those science-class models of an atom, with balls stuck on wires extending from a central sphere. There was even a Ronson shaver made with an atom motif design ($25).

Sheath

This shape is most often found in salt and pepper shakers made to look like cylinders with belts pulling them thinner in the center.

Space-Related

Flying saucers were a source of fascination as everyone looked toward the sky during the space race of the 1950s and 1960s. Other types of space-related motifs include the star burst, stars, the points of a compass, and rocket shapes in such forms as cocktail shakers. Similar to the star burst is the asterisk, which was also popular.

White flying-saucer lamp with bright pink, "sensitive" line (such as was typical of the period), $35.

Then there was the preoccupation with the satellite, as the first US satellites were launched during this period. Look for satellite-shaped plastic tape measures used to advertise Hoover vacuum cleaners ($18 each).

Push Button

Yet another name given to these years was the *Push-Button Era*. Push buttons were associated with military strength because of the common notion of defense missiles launched against Soviet attacks with the push of a button. Quite a few plastic household articles feature push buttons.

Handles

Handles were put on everything from early TV sets that weighed several hundred pounds to stereos—supposedly to make them more portable. Watch for recessed handles, which were especially popular.

The World's Fair

According to Thomas Hine, the end of the *Populuxe* era was the 1964 World's Fair, which was a rehash of things already available. Thoughts turned to serious social issues such as Civil Rights and the Vietnam War, and materialism became unpopular.

See Chapters 5 and 21 for World's Fair collectibles.

Part Two

WORKING PLASTICS

Little Green Sprout, green vinyl, jointed head, c1971, 6" tall, $12.

4

Advertising

Many of the collectibles in this chapter were issued as a form of direct advertising—that is, they were distributed to promote a particular company's services. Vinyl and plastic toys were especially popular as free premiums (in a cereal box, for instance) or as part of a "special offer" that the buyer had to mail away for. Charlie the Tuna is a good example of this kind of advertising.

Other advertising collectibles include any objects that are marked with some reference to a company other than a standard trademark. This includes containers or objects used as fixtures in a store, even though they may not have been intended as advertisements. In fact, many such items overlap into other chapters of this book, since advertisers put their logos, company names, or symbols on almost every conceivable type of object.

F. & F. Mold and Die Works made many of the products you'll encounter among these collectibles.

Charlie the Tuna, blue vinyl (marked 1973), made by The Product People, Minneapolis, MN, for Star-Kist Foods, Inc., $20. Rare.

Price Factors

Advertising collectibles normally bring respectable prices because of the interest in this field. Those issued by highly visible companies with a large collector following tend to bring especially good prices. Older products are usually rare (and therefore cost more) than comparable newer products, particularly since there were few such objects produced in the early years of this century, compared to hundreds of thousands, or even millions, produced today.

Good Prospects

Collecting relatively new promotional items, especially those distributed by well-known businesses, may be a good idea, as indicated by the rise of McDonald's collectibles.

McDonald's children's plates: winter, summer, spring, and fall scenes, 10" diameter, 1977, Lexington. Winter scene pictured, $6. (Fall also priced at $6.)

Vinyl Big Boy, 1974–1978, $8.

Advertising Dolls

Aim toothpaste, Smokey the Bear, R. Dakin and Co., Hong Kong, 8" tall, **$32**.

Campbell Soup Chef, vinyl squeak toy, 7" tall, **$40**.

Chicken of the Sea, vinyl mermaid, Shoppin' Pal by Mattel, 1970s, 14" tall, **$30**.

Cracker Jack Sailor, vinyl, Shoppin' Pal by Mattel, 1970s, 14" tall, **$28**.

Franco-American Spaghetti-O's (Campbell Soup Co.), The Wizard of O's, vinyl doll, 8" tall, **$15**.

Green Giant, Jolly Green Giant, made by The Product People of Minneapolis, MN, 9½" tall, **$25**.

Jack-in-the-Box moldable dolls: Jack, Secret Sauce Agent, Sleepy-Eyed Boy, **each, $20**.

Keebler Company, vinyl Keebler Elf, 1974, 6½" tall, **$15**.

Kellogg's Frosted Flakes, vinyl Tony the Tiger, 8" tall, **$20**.

Rice Krispies, Snap, Crackle and Pop vinyl squeak toys, c1975, 8" tall, **each $15**.

Kentucky Fried Chicken, Colonel Sanders, plastic nodder, 7" tall, **$35**, and Colonel Sanders, vinyl figure, **$20**.

Kitty Pan Litter, vinyl Glamour Kitty with cloth cape and crown, 7½" tall, **$9**.

Maypo Cereal, vinyl Marky Maypo, c1980, 10" tall, **$12**.

McDonald's dolls by Remco, made in Hong Kong, 1976.
a. Big Mac, **$20**.
b. Captain Cook, **$20**.
c. Hamburglar, **$20**.
d. Mayor McCheese, **$25**.
e. Professor, **$30**.
f. Ronald McDonald, **$29**.

Mobile Oil, foam latex doll, 5" tall, **$20**.

Vinyl Icee polar bear, red and blue on white, c1974, $12.

Pillsbury's Poppin' Fresh white vinyl dolls, 1970s.
Left to right:
a. Puppy, $12.
b. Poppin' Fresh, $10.
c. Poppie Fresh, $10.

Morton Salt, vinyl girl dolls wearing raincoats, blonde or brunette, 8″ tall, **each $20.**

Morton Salt, vinyl girl doll patterned after the original 1914 trademark, Shoppin' Pal by Mattel, 1970s, 14″ tall, **$25.**

Mr. Clean, vinyl, c1961, 8″ tall, **$25. *Rare.***

Munsingwear, vinyl penguin, 7″ tall, **$15.**

Nabisco, Donald Duck and Mickey Mouse 7 oz. cereal containers, 1966, **each, $45.**

Nestle Chocolate, vinyl Little Hans, 1969, 12½″ tall, **$25.**

Hoover Housewife holding a vacuum cleaner marked *Brother—You're strictly from Hoover,* **$30.**

Pepto Bismol, 24-Hour Bug Doll, green vinyl, 7″ tall, **$12.**

Pillsbury, Poppin' Fresh dolls, white vinyl, 1970s.
a. Cupcake (cat), **$12.**
b. Grandmommer, **$15.**
c. Grandpopper, **$15.**
d. House case, **$25.**
e. Poppin' or Poppie (fresh vinyl and cloth handpuppets in a biscuit can), **each, $18.**
f. Uncle Rollie and his car, **$35. *Rare.*** (The lights on the car open and close like eyes, and the rumble seat opens.)

Procter and Gamble, Pogo Series, **each, $10-$12.**

Ralston Purina, vinyl chuck wagon, 1975, **$10,** and Meow Mix vinyl cat, 1976, 4½″ tall, **$10.**

Sambo Restaurants, Sambo doll with huge eyes (from the story "Little Black Sambo"), 1972, 5″ tall, **$25.**

Sony Corporation, Sony Boy, 1960s, 8″ tall, **$10.**

Swanson International Dinners, International dolls, MIB, 8″ tall, **$10.**

Weatherbird Shoes red rooster bank, 3½″ × 4″, $10.

Red, doll-sized Coca-Cola cooler, $45.

Advertising Banks

Alka Seltzer, Speedy, **$25.**

A&P, pig bank, **$10.**

Curad by Kenner, Curad Taped Crusader, 1975, **$15.**

Eveready, cat bank, **$10.**

Kentucky Fried Chicken, Colonel Harland Sanders bank made by Starling Plastic, London, Canada, **$35.**

Pizza Hut, Pizza Pete, c1969, 7½″ high, **$15.**

Planter's Peanuts, Mr. Peanut, assorted colors, **$20.**

Quaker Oats, Cap'n Crunch, 7½″ high, **$20.**

RCA, Service Man, pale blue, 1960, 5″ high, **$30.**

Royal Gelatin, vinyl King Royal, 9½″ high, **$15.**

Miscellaneous

Not pictured: Good Humor, vinyl ice cream bar with a bite out, 1975, **$10.**

*Red Heinz bank with paper label, slot in rear, 7½″ high, $20. **Rare.***

*Yellow Fido and black Fifi sugar and creamer set, made by F. & F. Mold and Die Works of Dayton, OH, for Ken-L-Ration, c1950s, **set, $10.** (See the matching salt and pepper shakers in Chapter 5.) Not pictured: canister, **$22.***

Toy Coca-Cola dispenser in original box, $125.
Not pictured: *Pepsi dispenser, $45.*

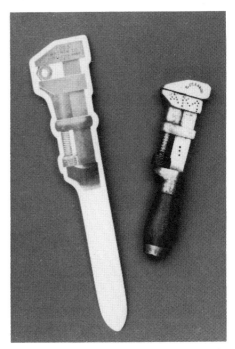

Celluloid letter opener made to advertise the real wrench, c1910, manufactured by the Coes Wrench Company. Letter opener, $45.

Holsum Bread dry measure (red), $3; red Firestone ice scraper, $3; ivory Celluloid bottle opener, $4.

McDonald's whistle on cord, $10.

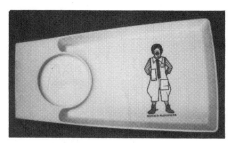

*White McDonald's snack tray picturing Ronald McDonald, **each, $10.***

*Store-display-size Mr. Peanut container for peanut bags, blue hat and transparent yellow face, paper label, **$45.***

*Mr. Peanut mug (green) and whistle (orange), **each, $15.** Not pictured: Mr. Peanut red, white and green blow pipe, **$8.***

*Yellow Pantry Pride hamburger maker, **$6,** and red, translucent, egg separator for poultry market, **$6,** both from the 1950s.*

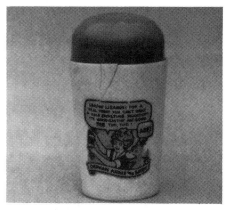

*Little Orphan Annie cold Ovaltine shake-up mug (Beetleware), made for The Wander Co. of Chicago, IL, 1930s, **$35–$40** (if in good condition). Not pictured: regular mug, **$28.***

*Yellow Shell toy truck with metal tank and rubber wheels, **$18.** Courtesy of the Westminster Clock Shop, Westminster, MD.*

Smokey the Bear toy canteen (brown) with paper eyes and a red vinyl strap, $25.

Red whiskey jug marked Windsor Supreme Canadian *(in gold paint),* **$10.**

1950s thermometer give-away from The Style Shoppe in New Bedford, MA, $18.

5

Kitchen and Serving Sets

Red Lustro-Ware canisters, Columbus Plastic Products, Columbus, OH, **set of 4, $30.** Not pictured: *Red Lustro-Ware canisters with white flowers,* **set, $20.**

Collectors of kitchen and dinnerware items tend to concentrate on sets. Scattered, one-of-a-kind items will not normally be as desirable, although Chapter 6 lists some notable exceptions.

At present, there seem to be more sets of kitchen items available in red than in any other color. Blue sets, on the other hand, are rare, and even more highly collectible.

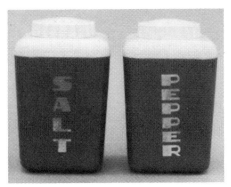

Block salt and pepper shakers (to match the canister set), **$18,** *are hard to find in good condition.*

Chef spice set (polyethylene) with shelf, **$45** (if complete—one figure is missing from the set pictured).

Flatware

Most of the flatware sets which qualify as plastic collectibles have plastic handles, but there are a few flatware pieces which are all plastic (see the cake and fruit knives pictured). Depending on what is combined with the plastic in the finished product, this flatware can command quite high prices.

Not pictured: Flatware, fish set, Celluloid and sterling silver, **8-piece set, $375.**

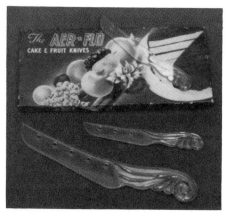

Streamlined Aer-Flo knives (with their original box), transparent plastic, **set of 3 with box, $20,** or individually, **each, $3.**

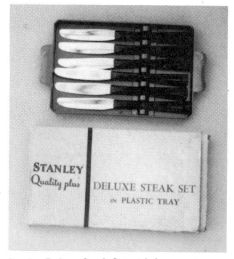

Stanley Deluxe Steak Set with brown, streamlined plastic handles and a plastic tray (in original box), Stanley Home Products, Westfield, MA, **set of 6, $22.**

Child's knife, fork, and spoon with butter-scotch Bakelite handles, **set of 3, $35.** Not pictured: *Regular flatware, butterscotch Bakelite handles with red dots,* **set of 8, $125.**

Ivory-colored, streamlined salad set with painted silver handles, **pair, $15.**

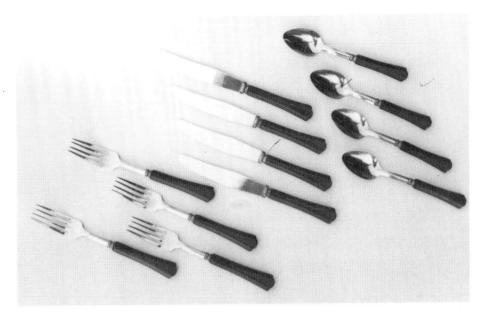

*Red-Catalin-handled flatware, **four 3-piece place settings, $65.***

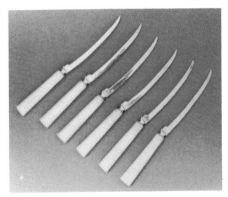

*Steak knives with ivory Celluloid handles, **set of 6, $35.** Not pictured: English carving set with plastic bone-look handles, Sheffield G. Parke and Sons, **3-piece set, $20.***

Plastics for Entertaining

From the 1920s through the 1950s, objects such as cocktail shakers were often used for parties and other entertaining. A new plastics collector looking for something different, elegant, and beautiful should consider streamlined examples of these, and look for the party-related sets that were popular during that time period as well.

Related sets include decanters and shot glasses, liquor sets, coasters, napkin rings, and drink stirrers. In particular, drink stirrers were especially popular during the Art Deco years and again in the 1950s. Look for top hats and white gloves (typically worn by "dandies" in the 1920s and 1930s) on the crests of these little sticks.

*Flower-shaped berry or salad set with large turquoise bowl, smaller pink ones, and matching pink utensils; Hofman Industries, Sinking Spring, PA, **set, $15.***

43

White coasters with painted gold removable spokes, the MP Coaster Corporation, **set of 6 and rack, $10.**

Plastic cup holders with tinted glass inserts, MIB, 2½" high, **set of 12, $45.**

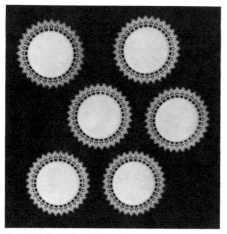

Lacy, pink, polyethylene coasters are unusual for plastic design; **set of 6, $8.**

Unusual, clear shot glasses with painted flamingoes and palm trees, **set of 4, $20.**

Embossed twig coasters: yellow, beige, red, and green, **set, $9.**

A pair of butterscotch, duck-shaped napkin rings; the one on the right is marbleized with green. **Each, $25.**

From the 1939 World's Fair, carved Bakelite napkin rings (blue) in the shape of the Trylon and Perisphere; they are also available in other colors such as orange. **Each, $30.**

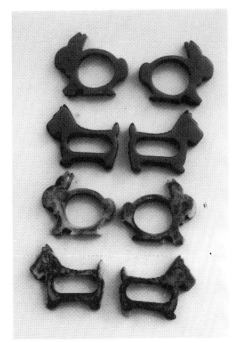

Bakelite rabbit- and Scottie-shaped napkin rings, four in red and four in marbled green, **each, $28.**

Bakelite napkin rings in a variety of colors.

Left to right:
a. Green or butterscotch, plain with a ribbed edge, ³⁄₄" wide, **each, $15.**
b. Brick, ³⁄₄" wide, **each, $18.**
c. Butterscotch, orange-red, Vaseline ¹⁄₂" wide, **each, $15.**

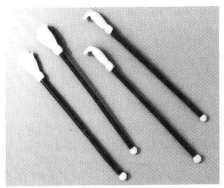

White gloves on tortoiseshell stirrers, **set of 4, $50.**

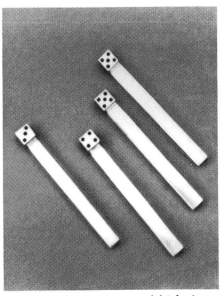

Acrylic and Bakelite dice-topped drink stirrers, **set of 4, $50.**

Celluloid sticks used to sweep the excess foam off of beer, **each, $25.**

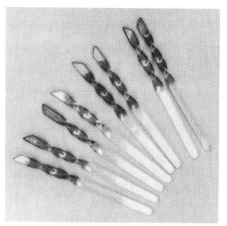

Tortoiseshell Ubangi stirrers, **set of 6, $20.**

Translucent drink stirrers, with lime, pink, blue, and yellow twisted tops, **set of 8, $38.**

Bakelite drink stirrers shaped like baseball bats (from the Jack Dempsey—Vanderbilt Hotel of Miami Beach, FL), **each, $20.**

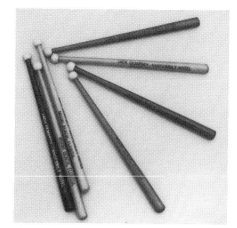

Salt and Pepper Shakers

Until John Mason invented his famous screw-top Mason jar, salt was served in dishes, and it was not until 1863 that the first screw-top salt shaker was patented. Since then, shaker sets have evolved into all manner of unusual shapes, and they're now a favorite among collectors. For instance, William Frank, of Westminster, Maryland—owner of 95 percent of the shakers in this chapter—is just one of thousands who collect them, and he has nearly 3000 different sets, many of them plastic.

In addition to the categories listed in the photographs which follow, there are a number of interesting types of shakers to look for. Humorous pieces are popular, as are hangers (two objects suspended from a third one) and companions (two objects sitting on a third one). There are even some shakers made like nodders, whose heads rock or bob, but they are rare.

Expect to see shakers shaped like animals, people, and objects. Bottles, for instance, are often used for advertising, and objects that complement each other are favorites—hammer and nail, cake and pie, mouse and cheese, and so on. As always, there's quite a bit of overlap among these groups, as you'll notice from the photographs.

Red, Catalin, rose-shaped salt and pepper shakers with metal mounts, **pair, $50. Rare.**

Advertising/Souvenir Shakers

Turquoise blocks decorated with shells and glitter (one is marked Florida*),* **pair, $3.** *Lanterns with translucent red globes on silver-looking bases,* **pair, $3.**

At left: 1939 World's Fair set in vibrant orange and blue Bakelite, Emeloid Co., Arlington, NJ, **pair, $25.** *Black and white torsos,* **pair, $25.**

Highly collectible plastic gas pumps representing the many different logos and color combinations made; some are marked USA. **Pair, $25.**

From the 1940s, Kool cigarette penguins Millie and Willie, **pair, $25.** *Pillsbury's Poppin' Fresh and Poppie, white vinyl,* **pair, $24.**

*Atlantic City souvenir combination set, transparent acrylic with embedded rose decoration, **pair, $5**. Musical celluloid shakers (black and gold) jingle as you season your food, **pair, $20**. **Rare**.*

*Mr. Peanut shakers in a variety of colors, **pair, $12–$18**.*

*Yellow Fido and black Fifi made to promote Ken-L-Ration dog food in the 1950s, common, **pair, $12**. (See the matching creamer and sugar in Chapter 4.) Also, black and white tube combination shaker sets with the Exxon tiger embossed on each end, **$5**.*

Appliance and Mechanical Shakers (with Movable Parts)

*Black jalopy set with red wheels that turn and people for removable shakers, common, **$12**. It's often purchased as a knickknack by collectors who aren't usually even interested in shakers.*

Red and white mechanical lawn mower with real rubber tires; salt and pepper shakers move up and down when the mower is pushed, **$25**. White mixer with shakers for beaters, **$14**.

Washer and dryer, pale green, **pair, $18**. TV set with shakers that lift out of the top, **$12**.

Left to right:
a. Silver-tone percolators with hand-painted flamingo, **pair, $8–$10**.
b. Motor-topped refrigerators, **pair, $25. Rare.**

Red, white, and gray wringer washer (the wringers are the shakers), **$14**. Tiny red toilets with lift-up lids, **pair, $8**.

Art Deco

Green Bakelite bullet-shaped shakers, marked Pachmayz, **pair, $30**. Blue urea combination set with black and white push buttons and hand-painted sailboat, marked Carvanite, **$28**.

Old sewing machine (brown and black) actually lifts out of its cabinet, **$28**.

Red shakers with hand-painted flower decoration, Plastic Novelties, Inc., of Los Angeles, CA, **pair, $10.**

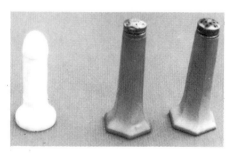

Left to right:
a. *Black and red "skyscraper" Celluloid set,* **pair, $35.**
b. *Black-topped Bakelite bullets with green base,* **pair, $30.**
c. *Marbleized red, 1½" high,* **pair, $32.**

Silver-look champagne bucket with removable salt and pepper bottles, **pair, $15.**

Bright yellow, red, and green croquet set complete with mallets, balls, and wickets, **$30.**
Rare. *At right: Plastic flower shakers sit on a ceramic log for an unusual combination,* **$5.**

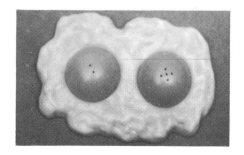

White bullet-shaped shaker, **$12,** *(if complete). Catalin shakers, 1930s,* **pair, $35.**

Whimsical companion set made to resemble a double-yoked, fried egg, **$12–$14.**

A few all-plastic hanging shakers: strawberries, $6; green grapes, $7; and corn, $8.

"Nobody's Perfect" companion set, with the two outer owls as removable shakers, $8.

A crossover item also sought after by snow dome collectors: Christmas snow dome (or snowball) combination, red and white plastic, $25. Rare.

Combination set featuring black and white guitar (with rubber strings) on a music stand, $15.

Additional Prices on Salt and Pepper Shakers

Aunt Jemima and Uncle Mose, made to promote Aunt Jemima pancake mix, mint, **pair, $60-$75.**

Art Deco salt and pepper shakers, green Bakelite with glass dome tops, 1930s, **pair, $30.**

Beatl marbleized set, **$30.**

Block shakers (kitchen-size) with orange and black butterfly decoration on a cream background, yellow lids, **pair, $10.**

Bone-look pipes, Hong Kong, **pair, $6.**

Flower shakers—plastic with metal mounted centers—and a metal frog as a bonus, **set of 3, $8.** *Rare.*

Loving cups in silver-tone plastic with paper label, souvenirs of Virginia, **pair, $5.**

Luzianne Coffee Mammy wearing a red skirt, Langniappe of N.O., USA, **repro, $75-$100.** (The earlier Luzianne Mammy, wearing a green skirt, F. & F. Mold and Die Works, **$150-$200.**

Strawberry and chocolate sodas set in silver-tone fountain-style holders, **pair, $7.**

Vinyl and hard plastic combination tiger, marked *Whirley Ind.*, 1974, **$8.**

6

Miscellaneous Kitchen Items

Some believe that collecting kitchen plastic items will someday rival Depression glass collecting. (In fact, the Philadelphia Museum of Art is collecting some 1970 cutlery from Ecko Plastics.) The field is vast; besides the sets of articles listed in Chapter 5, it includes dinnerware, tumblers, cooking utensils, picnic items, and other accessories.

Russel Wright melamine is an especially promising item in the kitchen collectibles category. It's valued at $5–$10 each for cup-and-saucer sets and for plates (sewing pieces are priced similarly). Other, less colorful designs are half value. Flea market prices, of course, will vary a good deal.

Among the trade/company names you'll see often in this field of collecting are Anchor Hocking, Fortune Brothers, Gothamware, MEDCO, Plas-Tex, Polyanne (from Chef's Aide), Rio, Shel-610, and Stanley (from Stanhome Products). Still others may be found in Appendix B, as well as in the descriptions for the items in this, and the previous, chapter.

As you look for kitchen objects, focus on the unusual ones and on those with patent dates (which can make an item worth more). Occasionally you can estimate the age of undated items by identifying some

Yellow Lustro-Ware bread box with hinged white lid, Columbus Plastic Products, Columbus, OH, $35.

Red and white cookie canister marked Lustro-Ware, *Columbus Plastic Products, Columbus, OH, $29.*

trend in their design; spangled items, for instance, are highly popular collectibles from the 1950s.

Spangled cups: brown, peach, and red, with embedded gold flecks; the coaster/lids have a molded, maple leaf design; **set, $24.** *(Subtract $1 for missing lid.)*

Tomato-shaped sauce boat with spoon, plus tomato- and pepper-shaped salt and pepper shaker set, all in red, **set of 3, $8.**

Good Prospects

As suggested, kitchen plastics offer a very promising future in collecting. You will find many items priced lower than listed here because so many persons are unaware of their value. In addition, only the truly avant-garde dealers are carrying them, so flea markets and yard sales are still great places to look for collectibles in this category. Remember: *Buy now—save later.*

Additional Prices

Bandalasta
a. Candlestick, marbleized, **pair, $60.**
b. Compote, marbleized, **$30.**
c. Cup and saucer, marbleized, **pair, $20.**
   Cup and saucer, plain, **pair, $10.**
d. Teapot, marbleized, **$65.**

Beatl
a. Cup and saucer, plain, **pair, $10.**
b. Luncheon plate, marbleized, **$20.**

Note: Prices of the urea products listed above may increase by as much as 25 percent for vibrant colors and good marbleizing, or decrease by as much as 25 percent when the colors are plain. In addition, an item intended as part of a set is worth more when it's found with the entire set.

Red, pierced plastic bread basket with hand-painted flower decoration, Plasmetl, **$3.**

Pale green, leaf-shaped candy dish with flamingo painted in the center, **$6.**

Cookie canister, red with white flowers, Lustro-Ware, Columbus Plastic Products, Columbus, OH, **$10.**

Drawer organizer (red), Plas-Tex, Los Angeles, CA, **$5.**

Turquoise ball jug, circle design, **$15.**

Household mixer, Lustro-Ware, Columbus Plastic Products, Columbus, OH, **$8.**

Syrup pitcher, red plastic lid with a metal insert, glass base, *A* logo, **$10.**

Syrup pitcher, turquoise plastic lid on a pressed glass base, Federal Housewares, Nibot Corp., Chicago, IL, **$9.**

Sugar shaker, red plastic lid with an Art Deco design, pressed glass base, Measuring Device Corp., NY, **$9.**

Pink and gray butter dish with roped edging, Plasmetl, **$4.**

Red ball jug with an Art Deco look, 6½" high, **$25.**

Bright yellow butter dish with colorful fruit molded onto the lid. **$9.**

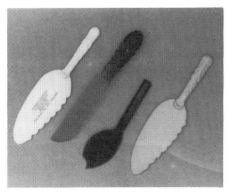

Cake and pie slicer/servers.
Left to right:
a. White with ad, Raubie's Grocery, Phone 35112, **$6.**
b. Translucent pink, **$6.**
c. Red Utility and Tomato Slicer/Server, **$4.**
d. Yellow with B logo, **$3.**

Square butter (or cheese) dish in peach plastic on gray, Plas-Tex Corp., Los Angeles, CA, **$10.**

Butterscotch- and lime green-handled cake breakers, **each, $15.**

Hand-painted urea cake server with tree design executed in oils; a push-button fork moves to hold the cake on the server, **$25.**

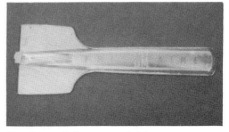

Translucent defroster wand, **$6.**

White, two-level chip-and-dip bowl with gold-tone metal rack, no mark, $12.

White-swirled five-cup flour sifter with red plastic handle, red rose decoration, $9.

Polyanne Knife Sharpener (pink), package marked Sharp-N-Hone *and* Chef's Aide, *$8.*

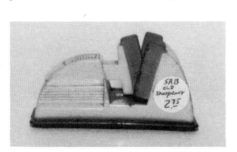

Cream urea knife sharpener was priced only $2.75 at PA flea market; current value, $10.

Salmon-colored spatter melamine, **each, $8.**

Pierced ivory napkin holder, hummingbird motif, 4½" high, **$10**.

Pink ball pitcher, textured, marked SPS, Canada, USA, **$10**, Smaller turquoise embossed pitcher, **$8**.

Molded plastic, three-section picnic plates, **each, $3**.

Lustro-Ware block pitchers (one in red and white and the other in green and white), original labels still intact, Columbus Plastic Products, Columbus, OH, **each, $15**.

Green Rio pitcher with streamlined design, USA, **$20**.

Art Deco bugle-lipped pitcher (salmon), marked Shel-Glo, USA, 8¼" high, **$30**.

Acrylic serving tray, heat-formed handles and glass insert with sandblasted design, 1940s, **$48.**

Salmon-colored triangular pitcher, marked It's Dripless, *Fortune Brothers, Northberge, NJ,* **$10.**

Creamy brown TV-snack tray with dividers for drinks, sandwiches, and extras; Columbus, Molded Plastics, Columbus, OH, **$10.**

Marbleized burgundy, black, and brown pitcher-and-tray set (possibly used in a motel with water glasses), Viceroy Plastics Co., Hudson, MA, **$30.**

Water pitcher with embedded gold spangles, **$18;** *and matching pie server,* **$6.**

7

Appliances and Gadgets

A lot of us tend to assume that because something is *electric*, it's also quite up-to-date. This is not necessarily the case. Some appliances from the 1930s and 1940s have become intriguing collectibles which in no way resemble the appliances we have today.

In part, this chapter features some Bakelite electrical appliances now sought by collectors. (A separate chapter each has been devoted to the lamp and radio categories, which have been especially popular.) Besides the ones included here, collectors are looking for fans, razors, televisions, and various novelty items, all with plastic casings.

Gadgets—from mousetraps to kitchen helpers to one-of-a-kind inventions—occupy the remainder of the chapter. Throughout history, Americans have been a creative lot, working to make things easier, quicker, or better, so there's a large, interesting assortment of these collectibles available. The catch is to find them in good condition.

As with other objects in this book, some of the gadgets overlap with another area. Most of them, in fact, would classify as kitchen items, but have been placed here because *gadgets* describes them more specifically.

One of a pair of beige record player speakers made to resemble satellite dishes, Philco, 1953, ***pair, $125.***

Car vacuum cleaner (notice the cord length), ***$45.***

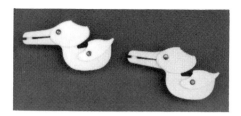

Celluloid blanket holders used to help keep baby covered, **pair, $30. Rare.**

Victor four-hole Choker Mouse Trap by the Animal Trap Co. of America, made of Bakelite, **$15.**

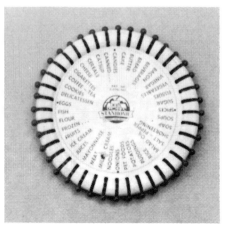

White and red grocery-shopping Memory Minder—clips lift to mark needed items— from Stanhome Products, **$8.**

Price Factors

Appliances

Colorful items often get the best prices, but well-designed brown Bakelite objects are also desirable.

Otherwise, be sure that the appliance is not cracked or severely scratched. In most cases, it should be in working condition to obtain full value.

Gadgets

A patent date on an item usually increases value because it indicates an approximate date of invention, and in most cases, the item's manufacturer. Although some objects continue to be manufactured years after the patent is issued, later objects have additional patent numbers to indicate improvements.

The first of anything, the prototype of an invention, or any item that shows a significant change in the way an object has been manufactured over the years can become valuable to a collector. Also look for the unusual, fun objects, either those you remember from childhood or recent ones that are good candidates for future collecting.

Bakelite 45 rpm record player, RCA Victor, 1950s, **$60 and up.**

Black and white Mark XII Imperial Flash camera, Herbert-George Co., Chicago, IL, $20.

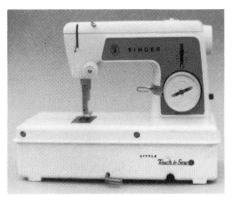

Little Touch & Sew toy sewing machine, Singer, works by battery or hand, $35. From the collection of Tony and Sandy Gatta, Westminster, MD.

Good Prospects

Undoubtedly, as more objects become computerized, many appliances that have been common for years will soon be outdated, and thus fair game for collecting. New gadgets are constantly being introduced (and old ones abandoned), making collectibles in this category even easier to identify.

W. C. Fields Red Nose Battery Tester with paper decoration; his nose lights up when the battery is good. American Noveltronics Corporation, 1974, $30.

Three-Dimension Viewer, Model E, View-Master Stereoscope, black, still in its original box with picture disks. Made by Sawyer's Inc., Portland, OR, 1950s, set, $30. Picture packets, each, $3; Disney packets, each, $10–$20.

Brownie Starlet camera, black, marked Limited London, Made in England, *Kodak, $20.*

Photo-Champ camera (uses 127 film), still in original box, 2½" × 3", $35.

Bright green and gray Bugs Bunny camera (uses Instamatic film), Helm Toy Corp., 1977, $35.

Kitchen Gadgets

Four silver-colored-leaf lids are raised when the acrylic plunger in the center of this candy dish is pushed. By Karoff, 4" × 4¾", $12.

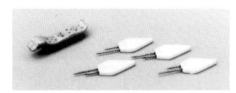

Jade green Catalin toothpick holder in the shape of a daschund, $35. Yellow Catalin corn holders, set of four, $32.

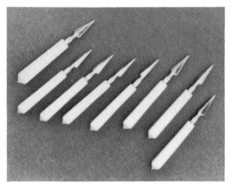

Corn holders with ivory Celluloid handles, set, $45.

Egg slicer (red) by MEDCO, New York, 3³/₄" l, **$4**.

Lady Betty Lunch-N-Bag, brown, with original box and thermos, Landers-Frary & Clark, New Britain, CN, **$25**.

Ice crusher, properly named The Jet, translucent plastic top (red) on a metal base, marked Daizy, St. Louis, c1948, **$25**.

Bakelite stand made to hold Celluloid menus and program cards. The white bear is marked The Roosevelt Bears; the butterscotch one, Midnight Suppers. Both are mounted on a black base. **$145**.

Pie server with butterscotch Catalin handle, **$20**.

Celluloid, recipe butler typical of the Art Deco period, red and black, **$60**.

Stainless steel Wit Whip with red and white plastic handle, Jo Wit Lab., New York, $12.

Red picnic set, all original, in its suitcase; Hemcolite Plastics. **Four place settings (including plates, cups, and flatware)**, **$145** (complete set). **Rare.**

Robert the Robot, acrylic, original design, 14" tall, **$150**. **Rare.**

Assorted carved Bakelite bracelets (left to right): matched cream and brown, 1/4" wide, **pair, $30**; ivory with arrow design, 1/2" wide, **$22**; dark olive green, 3/4" wide, **$35**; dark orange-red, elaborate, 1" wide, **$42**; bright red, 1/2" wide, **$25**; marbleized olive green, 3/4" wide, **$20**; brown, 3/4" wide, **$35**.

Celluloid hair combs, Art Deco, 1920s (left to right): Butterscotch with green rhinestones, **$50**; black with clear rhinestones, **$60**; black with painted red accents and cutout bird design, **$55**.

Sheaffer pens and pencils

Left to right:
a. *1929 pencil, Jade Radite, chain attached to ribbon ring,* **$100.**
b. *1929, #3-25, Red Radite, GF trim,* **$195.**
c. *1928, #5-30, Jade Radite with Black and GF trim, ribbon ring,* **$100.**
d. *1924 Lifetime, BCHR, GF trim, long straight clip,* **$425.**
e. *1926 Lifetime, Pearl and Black Radite, GF trim,* **$145.**
f. *1928 Lifetime pencil, Pearl and Black Radite, GF trim,* **$125.**
g. *1928 Loaner pen, #6 nib, Red Radite,* **$400.**
h. *1928 Lifetime, Jade Radite, GF trim,* **$100.**
i. *1922 Lifetime, BCHR, GF trim,* **$135.**
j. *1927 Lifetime pencil, Jade Radite,* **$95.**

Bottom:
k. *1926 Purple self-filling pen box,* **$20.**
l. *1928 Lifetime, Green Radite, GF trim,* **$100.**
m. *Same as l.*

Note the Celluloid's color deterioration in examples l and m.

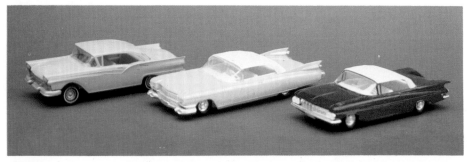

Snap-together models: 1957 Ford, lime green, **$15;** *1958–59 Cadillac, yellow,* **$20;** *1959 Chevrolet, red,* **$20.**

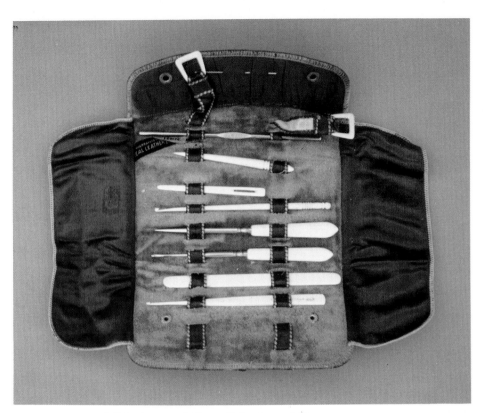

*Crochet set; cream Celluloid in a royal blue, gold-lined case, **$40**.*

*Bakelite calendar holder with metal Springer Spaniel on marbelized butterscotch base, **$65**.*

Twenty-two-piece Celluloid dresser set in pearlized butterscotch (the most complete I have ever seen): vases, **pair, $35;** picture frames, **pair, $40;** hair receiver and powder box, **$20;** beveled mirror, **$12;** nail accessories, **each $3–$5;** tray, **$12;** dresser clock, **$18;** crystal perfume bottle in Celluloid container (ground stopper), **$45;** comb and brush, **set, $12;** shoehorn, **$6;** scissors, **$15;** individual box, **$15;** and clothing brush, **$8.**

The entire set is worth more as a rare unit—**$250.** Smaller matched groups within the set are also worth more. Note: Subtract 25 percent of the values listed if the items are cream-colored.

Heavy Bakelite link bracelets, ½" wide: one color, **$125;** two colors, **$150.**

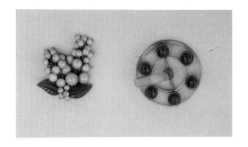

Translucent butterscotch belt buckle with green accents, **$29.** Pin, dangling yellow oranges against carved Bakelite leaves (green), **$70.**

Hat pin topped with two cherries; butterscotch, red, and green Bakelite, **$185.** Matching earrings, **pair, $75.** Strawberry bar pin, **$257 (rare).**

Reverse-carved jewelry: dress clips, **each, $20;** pins, **each, $75;** buckles, **each, $30;** rings, **each $40.**

Dotted Bakelite bracelets, **each $200.**

Orange Celluloid belt with ivory Celluloid cameo medallions including full-color illustrations on each cameo, **$150.**

Red and black Bakelite cherry necklace, $250. Horse head pin, hand-carved, red Bakelite, $75. Red and black Bakelite bar pin, belt design, $125.

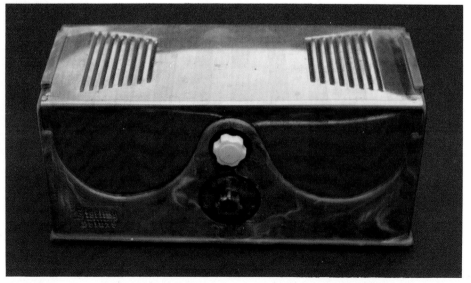

Sterling Deluxe, marbleized blue and white with chrome shield on top, c1949, $135.

*First Communion prayer book, cream Celluloid with pastel illustration on the cover, c1905, **$35**.*

*Pearlized ivory Tuskeloid (Celluloid) clock with butterscotch trim, New Haven Clock Co., **$35**.*

*Art Deco bookends, transparent resin balls and butterscotch Bakelite bases, **$85**.*

*Bakelite Fada radio, butterscotch with red trim, Art Deco style, **$1100**.*

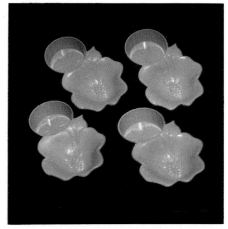

*Pink nut-and-drink coaster/server set (also by Hofman Industries, Sinking Spring, PA) comes in red as well, **each, $2**.*

*Liquor ball, marbleized chocolate with chrome push-top dispenser and six glasses, **set, $65**.*

71

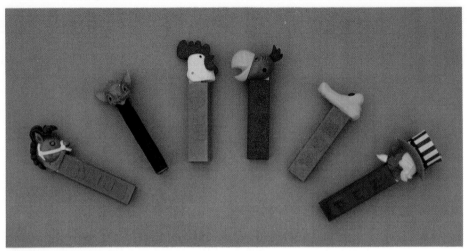

Pez candy containers (left to right): *horse, Austria, $20; fawn, Austria, $10; rooster, Austria, $15; parrot, Austria, $15; alligator, Austria, $50; Uncle Sam, Austria, $55.*

Circle bracelet, necklace, and earrings made of caramel, red, black, brown, ivory, and burgundy Bakelite pieces, $225. Matching horseshoe pin, laminated Bakelite (christened "Super Jewelry" by one dealer), $200.

8

Lamps

If you think lamps are just necessary electrical fixtures that clutter your room with ugly stray cords, take a look at the amazing variety of interesting plastic ones. Homemade pink acrylic elephants, black and butterscotch Bakelite poles, 1950s and 1960s flying saucer lamps, and uniquely designed nursery lamps become the focal point of a room rather than fitting inconspicuously into a corner. Many collectors prize these plastic lamps almost as they would an art object.

Cream-colored urea bracket lamp, **$30.**

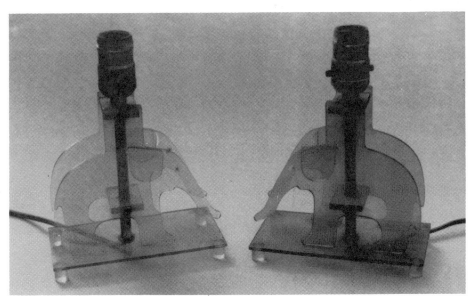

Handmade acrylic elephant lamps, **pair, $125.**

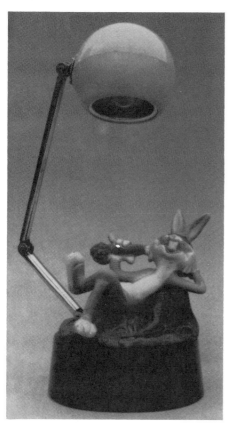

Satellite-style lamp reminiscent of 1950s–1960s interest in outer space, **$25.**

High-intensity Bugs Bunny lamp (in bright green, yellow, and gray), **$35.**

Baltimore Colts Helmet lamp, 1973, Pro Sports Marketing, Inc., Concord, CA, **$65.**

Price Factors

As you examine a lamp, consider that electrical problems are usually cheap to repair. If the lamp doesn't work, you might even get a better buy than if it were in good condition, because a low repair cost added to the unusually low asking price will probably not equal its actual value.

Otherwise, pay special attention to Catalin lamps in color, which are bringing high prices at shows. In fact, many are now rare.

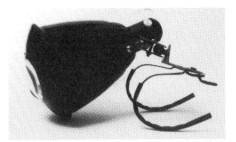

*Bakelite bed lamp with Art Deco accents, **$20**.*

*Butterscotch and black Bakelite, **$280**.*

*Bakelite bed lamp (brown) with magnifying glass over the bulb, Atlas Consolidated Corp., Brooklyn, NY, **$25**.*

*Bakelite lamp with typical Art Deco lines, **$22**.*

*Bakelite desk lamp (brown) with molded pen and paper clip holders, common, **$30**.*

Good Prospects

Right now, interest in objects from the 1950s and 1960s is just growing, so these should make wise investments. Pink lamps, for instance, are good for creating the 1950s look.

Acrylics have also been overlooked up to this point, and could become especially valuable (see the "Price Factors" section of Chapter 10).

Pink bed lamp with streamlined look, marked Eagle, $22.

Brown bed lamp (1950s–1960s) with dart design (imitating aircraft wings) on the metal light reflector, Rex Mfg. Corp., 8″ × 3¾″, $18.

Pink bed lamp with metal decoration and light filter, 12″ × 5″, $18.

Heat-twisted acrylic lamp, $38.

76

9

Radios

Most of the radios pictured in this chapter are photographed courtesy of Paul Mintz and Arleen Goodrich, of Baltimore, Maryland, and Dharam Damama Klalsa, of Los Angeles, California.

Although the radio was developed in the late 1880s, its Golden Age did not arrive until 1925, and it only lasted until 1950, when television stole the spotlight. Yet the fervor of the ensuing collecting trend suggests that the radios from this period will not soon be forgotten. Plastic radios from the 1930s, for instance, are actually selling higher than some of the period's furniture. Even lower-priced radios occupy an impressive $65–$100 range.

Tom Thumb automatic radio made of brown Bakelite and trimmed in fabric, c1948, **$100.**

Bendix Aviation Corporation, black and marbleized green, **$600–$800.**

Majestic, featuring strong vertical lines, c1938–1939, **$75.**

Price Factors

Collectors paying such high prices expect a cabinet in good condition. They are less interested in whether the radio works or not. Less expensive radios are often purchased by noncollectors as novelties for their homes, in which case they are expected to be in good operating condition.

Vibrant green radio with AC/DC receiver, marked Sparton Radio/Television, *c1950, the Sparks Wittington Co., $75.*

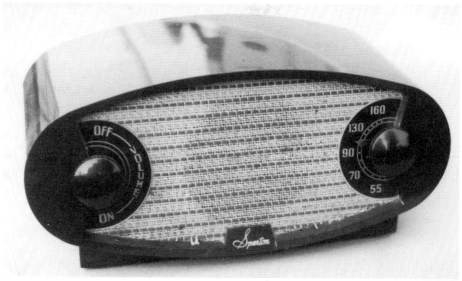

Burgundy Sparton, c1946, $85

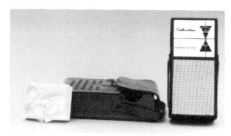

Sears Silvertone transistor radio (black) with real leather case, c1959, $30.

Blue clock radio by Bulova, c1952, $45.

Stewart Warner (1950s), brown Bakelite, still a bargain at $45.

General Electric clock radio from the 1950s, pale pink with a black face, $35 in good condition. (Watch out for chips, fading, and cracks.)

Red is perhaps the most valuable single color available; two-tone radios are also popular. Keep in mind that many colors used for plastic radios tend to fade. You can check for this by removing the knobs. (If you're displaying a radio at a show, just remove the knobs yourself and keep them in a different place so that no one will walk away with one of them, absentmindedly or otherwise.) You can also see some of the radio's original color on the back. Radios that have not faded can be worth more than those that have, especially if their original color is an attractive, rich tone. Marbleized Bakelite, which collectors commonly refer to by the trade name *Catalin,* also creates a look prized by collectors.

Red Coca-Cola radio shaped like a cooler, $750.

Red Sylvania radio, 1950s, **$50.**

Emerson, marbleized red with pearlized white grill, **$3000.** Not pictured: *Addison shortwave, black-green Bakelite with butterscotch trim and marbleizing, c1938,* **$2000.** (See also the radio pictured on the front cover.)

Red General Electric (1950s) with a Deco-look metal-rimmed face, **$65.**

Radio camera, marked BELL *Kamra, red with silver trim, c1955–1959, made in Japan,* **$100.**

Emerson Patriot, marbleized olive with brown accents, **$800–$1500.**

Motorola (1950s), bold red with Bakelite trim, **$65.**

Emerson's Little Miracle (butterscotch) with its original box, **$1000.**

Fada, Model 711, butterscotch Catalin with a marbleized olive cast; the box has probably been affected by light over the years (as is often the case with Bakelite), $500.

Fada Bullet, Bakelite, marbleized dark green with butterscotch trim, 1934, butterscotch, $1000.

Finally, watch for interestingly shaped radios. The Art Deco bullet is a classic example of their popularity.

Note: Max Alth's *Collecting Old Radios and Crystal Sets* (Wallace-Homestead Book Company) contains a patent date listing that will help you date your radio collection. See the Bibliography for details of publication.

Motorola with maze-looking face, green Bakelite centered on brown, c1948–1950, $100.

Emerson Tombstone (note its shape), 1937, butterscotch Bakelite, $1500; blue or red, $8000 and up.

White urea radio with small amounts of green and black marbleizing, c1938–1940, probably a Truetone made by Trevose TV and Appliance Co., Trevose, PA, $225.

81

*Building-shaped Zenith in brown Bakelite with contrasting white buttons, c1936, **$125**.*

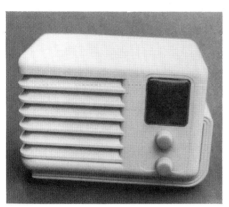

*A collector's favorite: Philco Transitone, brown Bakelite, c1948, **$175**.*

*Mirror-Tone, Bakelite with white, baked-on finish, **$45**.*

White Mickey Mouse clock radio, General Electric, $60.

Good Prospects

Children's radios, like the Mickey Mouse one pictured here, are already finding their way into collections, even if they are of recent manufacture. Hold on to similar TV and movie character-related items.

Advertising radios are promising collectibles, as well as unusual shapes that are new. The new streamlined stereo radios, with their unusual colors, are other good possibilities.

Character Radios for Children:
Exxon tiger, **$25.**

Spiderman (red), **$30.**

Talking Batman, **$35.**

Talking Raggedy Ann and Andy, **$28.**

10

Timepieces

Just as plastic clocks caused people to marvel at the advances made from early timekeeping devices such as sundials, water clocks, and hourglasses, increasingly innovative contemporary clocks are beginning to make the older plastic ones a source of fascination. The broad range of styles available in these clocks should prove as interesting to collectors as their old-fashioned mechanics.

*Speckled green Celluloid clock with molded columns and cream trim; United States patent dated April 27, 1920; 8" high, **$30.***

*General Electric pedestal clock, pink, **$22.***

Cream Celluloid Art Deco clock marked Telealarm Jr., *Warren Telechron Inc., Ashland, MA, **$28.***

Red and white General Electric Telechron,
$22.

*Brown Bakelite skyscraper-style alarm clock
(also shows day and date of month), marked*
AM BAG & BURLAP CO., Hammond Clock
Co., Chicago, IL, **$45.**

*MinitMaster Jr. electric timer, white quilted
plastic with red and white dial,* **$20.**

*An early digital clock, marbleized brown,
marked* TELE-VISION, *the Tele-Vision Clock
Corp., Pittsburgh, PA,* **$30.** From the collec-
tion of Vince Viore, Westminster, MD.

Price Factors

Purer colors such as ivory tend to get lower prices than exotic ones like marbleized jade green or fiery red. If two clocks are of similar colors, or if they are of common colors—an ivory Celluloid and a brown Bakelite, for instance—the Bakelite clock will normally sell for more money. On the other hand, if the Celluloid clock is rare, of unusual design, or more exceptional than the Bakelite in some other way, it will command the higher price.

Butterscotch Bakelite Telechron Alarm also tells the day and date; Warren Telechron Inc., Ashland, MA, $30.

Time Master, Celluloid with marbleized green columns and radium dial, made in Germany, $65.

Marbleized green Celluloid dresser clock, the Lux Clock Manufacturing Co., $30.

Cream Celluloid Ingersoll alarm clock, $20.

General Electric Telechron, clear acrylic with brass numbers around the face, $95.

Acrylics vary somewhat in price, with suburban areas preferring more contemporary styles than are popular in a country setting. In general, however, the Art Deco look is sweeping the country, and since acrylic pieces look great with Deco, acrylics everywhere are expected to rise steadily in value. If this material achieves the popularity expected, prices on acrylic clocks may even skyrocket because of their rarity. Plus, acrylic scratches easily, so fine-quality items will be highly sought by collectors. Finally, acrylic items are often handmade, which means that an acrylic clock might be a one-of-a-kind art object, and more valuable as such.

Novelty clocks (and watches) are another popular group to watch for. Unlike pens, which are collector-specific (primarily collectors pay the high prices for them), novelty clocks appeal to everyone. Whether they buy a 36-inch Mickey Mouse wall clock shaped like a wristwatch, or a collection of comical clocks whose eyes and/or tails move as they tick, a lot of people simply consider novelty clocks fun to own. Thus, there are more prospective buyers, and higher prices result.

Lighted waterfall clock creates the impression of water flowing over the waterfall and a burning fire in the background. Master Crafters Clock Corp., Chicago, IL, $40.

Art Deco clock in ivory cellulose acetate (Lumarith); the light inside flashes as the alarm rings. Westclox, $30. From the collection of Arleen Goodrich, Baltimore, MD.

Ship's wheel electric clock, Bakelite and brass-plated, Warren Telechron Inc., Ashland, MA, $40. This was a wedding present to my mother during the 1940s.

White church clock; the bell ringer in the base moves and rings the bell above as the clock lights up, $35 (in good condition). Courtesy of the Westminster Clock Shop, Westminster, MD.

Good Prospects

Save those now-cheap children's plastic digital watches with popular emblems such as football team mascots, or those which feature popular characters such as Miss Piggy. Save similar clocks as well.

Any current novelties—for example, talking clocks for children—should be worth considering.

Additional Prices

Baby Ben, dresser style, cream Celluloid, **$27.**

Electric steeple clock, brown Bakelite, Waterbury, **$50.**

General Electric's Telechron; chocolate Bakelite with Art Deco styling, metal base, and octagonal shape, **$110.**

Sessions electric alarm clock, cream Celluloid, **$28.**

Cream Celluloid dresser clock in working condition, $25.

Turquoise Panelescent by Sessions, $15.

11

Miscellaneous Household Items

Household items have been made from a number of plastics, including fiberglass and some rare acrylics. Although the household category could include substantially large pieces of furniture, this chapter basically deals with the smaller items, which appear to be the best candidates for collecting.

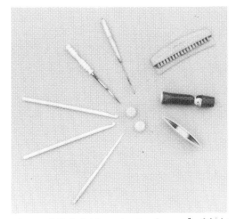

Assorted Celluloid crochet hooks, **each, $4.** *At right: Red and ivory Celluloid figure for holding pins and needles (cap unscrews to become a thimble),* **$10.** *Thread winder and brush,* **each, $10.**

Gothamware clothes sprinkler, green and yellow, **$9.**

Bakelite record holder with embossed battle scene, c1916, **$100. Rare.**

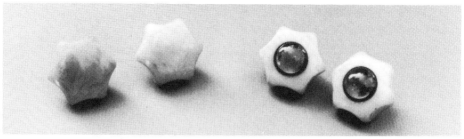

*Butterscotch Bakelite water faucet handles: plain, **pair, $65;** with red studs, **pair, $100.***

*Celluloid picture frame with four-way easel, 1950s, 8" × 10", **$50.***

*Marbleized light green sewing box—its clear lid is decorated with embossed sewing needs; Hommer Mfg. Co., Newark, NJ; common, **$12.** (Also comes in other colors and motifs.)*

*Coronet pin cushion in original box: The top of the crown—green velour set in a gold plastic base—lifts off to reveal a sewing box; E.F. Lawrence and Co., Inc., Northboro, MA, **$20.** Dog tape measure (Celluloid), **$45.***

*Large tortoiseshell sewing box with three sections that swivel out for use, topped with a molded rib design and gold-colored medallion, **$30.***

In General

Choice picture frames in heat-twisted acrylic are still low in price. Also look for planters and related objects—especially the *wire* ones (those made to rest on metal stands), which are currently in great demand with collectors in the Baltimore/Washington area. Matching wire furniture has been equally successful.

Flower frog (red); Hommer Mfg. Co., Newark, NJ; 7¹/₄" in circumference; $12.

Mirror-backed, marbleized burgundy shadow-box, $25. **Rare.**

Flower frog (white and green) in original box, Twinco, England, $15.

*Cone-shaped fiberglass planters (made between 1945 and 1960) with welded wrought-iron legs; available in pink, blue, yellow, green; **pair, $140.** From the author's collection.*

Demaree Molded Plastic three-footed planter, multicolored (grays, browns, and cream), Kokomo, IN, $8.

*White urns with painted gold trim, Carlisle Mfg. Co., Newark, NJ, 8" high, **pair, $13**.*

Ceramic *wall pockets*, or planters that hang on the wall, have recently become popular in the antiques market. Now the plastic wall pockets, several of which are included here, are gaining attention.

*Wall pocket, green with molded flower design around rim (also available in red), Ardel Products, **$6**.*

Vanities

Expensive vanity sets were customary wedding presents in the early 1900s. But the introduction of Pyralin (Celluloid) vanities made attractive sets affordable to almost everyone. Such vanities were made to resemble a variety of more expensive materials such as tortoiseshell and ivory, and given luxurious-sounding names such as *French Ivory* to obscure the fact that they were imitations. Now that they are no longer in demand for practical uses, they have become quite collectible.

*Bellows wall pocket, yellow with rose decoration, **$12**.*

*Celluloid-topped hair receiver and pressed-glass powder jar, **pair, $28**.*

Celluloid dresser set including one box with a beveled mirror mounted in brass, and another with a caramel divided tray. Each is black with a pearlized lid and black and gold Deco-style decorations. **Set, $45.**

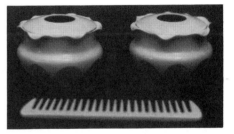

Celluloid hair receivers, **pair, $20;** *extra large Celluloid comb,* **$10.**

Jade green Celluloid Art Deco dresser set; includes tray with lace insert, brush, comb, mirror, and nail buffer, **$75.** *Not pictured: Bandalasta Ware (urea) dresser set, marbleized blue,* **$95.**

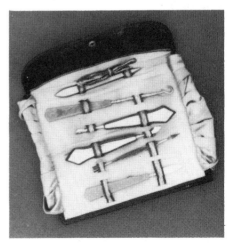

Traveling manicure set, pearlized pink and white Celluloid, **set of 6, $20.**

Imitation tortoiseshell (Celluloid) dresser set, **$45.**

Celluloid vanity items are nearly as varied as the silver-plated ones made in the late nineteenth century: There are nail cleaners, rouge boxes, nail files and buffers, hair receivers (in which women saved hair for use in hair crafts), powder boxes, vases, clocks, ring boxes, dresser trays, hand mirrors, and combs. The most common (and therefore, usually least expensive) colors are off-white (referred to here as cream) and ivory (a more yellowed white), deemed appropriate colors for the new bride. Green, marbled green, butterscotch, and tortoiseshell are also common, while pumpkin and torquoise are quite unusual.

Cream Celluloid comb in a torquoise, black, and cream marbleized case on a grosgrain ribbon, 1920s–1930s, $35.

Celluloid folding comb in the Art Deco style, cream and black with a clown decoration, 1920s–1930s, $30.

Ivory and cream Celluloid set, including brush, $10; button hook, $8; and cuticle cutter, $5.

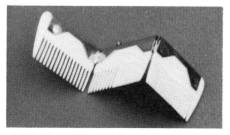

Celluloid metal-mounted comb made to fold in sections, Germany, $25.

*Catalin-topped glass perfume vials in green, butterscotch, and dark orange, **each**, $20.*

Purse perfume bottles in transparent acrylic with embedded rose decorations in black acrylic tops, **each, $15.**

Hand-painted scent boxes, 1920s, France, **each, $32.** *Red Bakelite perfume-holder necklace (contains a tiny glass vial),* **$70.**

The plainer of these items bring the lowest prices. In comparison, objects that have been decorated, embossed, or otherwise enhanced—perhaps with lace and metal mounts—may cost more, especially if they have good Art Deco lines. Normally a single item in an intact set would be proportionately worth more than an individual one that couldn't be matched. The more items in the set, and the more interesting they are, the more the set should be worth.

Blown-glass perfume bottle and its cream Celluloid holder with marbleized pink and black decoration, Germany, **$48.**

Trademark First Class toothbrushes in their original box, cream Celluloid, Imperial Brush Factory, Osaka, Japan, **set, $35. Rare.** From the collection of Vera Leister, Westminster, MD.

Butterscotch compact with sterling silver clasp and powder puff marked Ton-Ton, *1940s,* **$28.**

*Green Catalin manicure set with green and black marbleized Celluloid box; the cylinder unscrews to store the tools, **set, $35.***

*Urea Trio-ette compact (with original box) in three sections: powder, mirror (center), and lipstick handle, **$32.***

Razors

Straight-edge razors, which continued to be popular during the early twentieth century despite the invention of safety razors, have also outlived their usefulness to become plastic collectibles. You will see many Celluloid ones made to imitate ivory or tortoiseshell. Those with beautiful designs are worth more than plain ones, and those in their original cases or with advertisements on the blade are particularly good finds.

A variety of men's toiletries, including shaving accessories, safety razors (the hoeshaped variety common today), and even their Art Deco boxes are also on the market for interested collectors.

*Blue Celluloid Art Deco hand mirror with black accents, **$22.***

Celluloid straight razors: black, marked Torrey Razor Co., *Worchester, MA, **$30;** cream, **$12.***

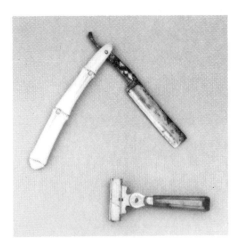

GEM safety razor with the "New GEM Micro-matic Singledge Blade," in a burgundy urea Art Deco box, $20 (complete).

Bamboo design Celluloid straight razor, Camillus Cuttery Co., NY, $20. Butterscotch Catalin-handled razor with gold-plated head, Schick Injector, $12. Not pictured: Figural straight razors—Eagle, $125; man on horse, $160; nude, $95; sailboat, $230.

Caramel Catalin comb and brush set with engraved metal decoration, set of 3, $18.

Non-Electric Viceroy Dry Shaver (in original box), brown Bakelite, the Rolls Razor Limited Co., England, $22.

Oval Celluloid brush with real bristles, black and ivory, Harriet Hubbard Ayer, Inc., $9.

Every-Ready shaving brush with real bristle and screw-on case in black and cream Celluloid, $15.

Good Prospects

Vanities. Look for those unusual razors from the 1950s and 1960s, electric razors in weird colors and styles, and even the first disposable razors as good possibilities for future collecting.

General. The Philadelphia Museum of Art has acquired modern plastics as part of its collection. Among its collection is an early-seventies plastic umbrella stand designed and made in Italy (in addition to the cutlery mentioned at the beginning of Chapter 6). If this is any indication of the future of collectible household plastics, collectors need to stay alert in order to identify sleepers in this category.

Made-Rite Shaver holder, razor, and pure-bristle brush; ivory and red barber pole stripes and black accents, 6¹/₂" high, $35. From the collection of Betty McNulty, Westminster, MD.

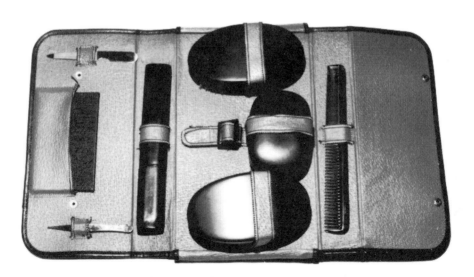

Men's travel set (black Celluloid) in a real leather case, $40 (if complete—one piece is missing from the set shown).

Streamlined urea shoehorns in prune and ivory, **each, $14.**

Men's travel set; leather case contains Celluloid wood-grain accessories, a stand-up mirror, and a burgundy Celluloid soap dish, **$40.** Courtesy of the Westminster Clock Shop, Westminster, MD.

Folding brown-and-black-striped Celluloid shaving mirror with milk-glass insert and shaving brush with real bristle, **$65.** Courtesy of the Westminster Clock Shop, Westminster, MD.

12

Fountain Pens

Fountain pen collecting is fast becoming a widely recognized hobby. A friend of mine recently attended a major show in Chicago devoted solely to pens.

Why have pens become so popular? Perhaps it is the interesting innovations, made during the last 100 years, which have brought us from the feather-clip pen to the modern roller ball and ballpoint pens of today. But one sure reason is collectors' fascination with the bright colors that first became available with the help of Pyralin plastics.

Exotic Colors

In 1924, Sheaffer was the first to introduce Du Pont's Pyralin (cellulose nitrate, or Celluloid) in pen form. Their marbleized jade green beauty started a trend that gave a tremendous boost to the pen industry, as companies were able to attract customers with colors and designs they had never dreamed possible.

Before then, rubber pens had been available in a very limited number of colors. Suddenly, every color combination imaginable seemed possible, and the companies created names to match the appeal of the

Artist's pens, Bakelite (butterscotch, black, and two shades of green), **set, $60.** See Chapter 13 for examples of other Bakelite pens.

colors. Exotic names like Wahl-Eversharp's Kashmir Green and Morocco evoked images of faraway places. Parker followed suit with Mandarin Yellow and Lapis Blue, the latter relying on the imagery of semiprecious stone. Still other colors were vividly defined with names such as Cardinal Red (for an orange-red shade), and so on.

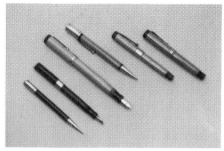

Parker Duofolds

Left to right:

a./b. 1928 Duofold pencil and pen, Lapis Lazuli Blue, GF trim band, ribbon rings, **set, $360.**

c./d. 1927 Big Red (Duofold Sr.) pen and pencil, **set, $550.**

e. 1927 Duofold Jr., Chinese Red, GF trim band, **$175.**

f. 1928 Duofold Jr., Chinese Red, GF trim, **$145.**

Ad for the Parker Duofold De Luxe in Moderne Black & Pearl (introduced in 1927) and Lapis Lazuli Blue (1928)

Parker Duofolds (including button fillers)

Left to right:

a. 1927 Duofold De Luxe Sr., Black and Pearl, GF trim, button filler, **$475.**

b. 1928 Duofold Sr., Lapis Lazuli Blue, GF trim, button filler, **$845.**

c. 1928 Duofold Jr. pencil, Lapis Lazuli Blue, GF trim, **$170.**

d. 1928 Duofold Sr., Jade, GF trim, button filler, **$375.**

e. 1928 Duofold Sr. pencil, Jade, GF trim, **$375.**

f. 1928 Duofold Jr. pencil, Jade, GF trim, **$170.**

g./h. 1928 Duofold Sr. pencil and pen, Black, GF trim, button filler pen, **set, $575.**

1931 Wahl-Eversharp Pyralin Pens

Left to right:

a. Oversized decagonal (10-sided) pencil, Coral (red), 5¾" long, **$175.**

b. 1925 oversized decagonal pencil, Sapphire Blue, 5¾" long, **$195.**

c./d. Miniature Equipoised pen and pencil set, Jade and Pearl, 3¾" long, **$85.**

e. Miniature doric, Morocco, **$30.**

f. Pencil, Blue Pearl, **$35.**

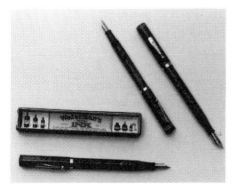

Below the box: *1928 #7 hard rubber Red Ripple Waterman with purple nib; with original box, $385.*

Top left: *#5 HR Red Ripple with red nib, $265, and 1928 #7 HR Red Ripple with pink nib, $375.*

1935 Wahl-Eversharp Dorics (12-sided Pyralins)

Left to right:

a. *Cathay (pearlized-green-lined), #7 adjustable nib with Safety Ink Shut-Off, GF trim, $375.*

b. *Pencil, Jet Black, $125.*

c. *1937 Burma (pearlized dark gray), Safety-Ink Shut-Off, chrome-plated trim, $375.*

d. *Pencil, Pearlized Burma, chrome-plated trim, $150.*

Also pictured: *1933 pencil, Cathay (green), square lead, GF trim, $150.*

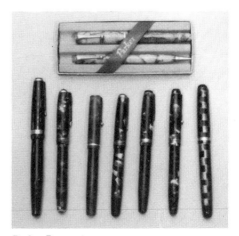

Parker Permanites

Top: *1935 pen and pencil set (original box), Onyx, GF trim, button filler, $200.*

Left to right:

a. *1944 Blue Diamond Vacumatic, Green and Brown, Pearl and Black stripes, GF trim, vacuum filler, $95.*

b. *1947 Vacumatic; Green, Pearl, and Black; GF trim; vacuum filler, $85.*

c. *1935 Duofold, Green and Bronze, GF trim, button filler, $140.*

d. *1936 De Luxe Challenger; Silver, Pearl, and Black; nickel-filled trim; button filler, $85.*

e. *1936 Challenger: Green, Pearl, and Black; GF trim, $95.*

f. *1932 Duofold; Red, Pearl, and Black marbled; GF trim, $270.*

g. *1943 Duofold, Red and Black checkerboard pattern, GF trim, button filler, $200.*

Marbled and pearlized models became especially popular. Waterman's Nacre, a black and pearl combination, was one of the most beautiful of all, shimmering like mother-of-pearl in the light.

Soon, other pen companies were forced to follow Sheaffer's lead in adopting the colorful Pyralin. Sheaffer coined the term *Radite* for its plastic, while Parker called it *Permanite*. Technically, it was all the same material. The fact that this new substance was virtually nonbreakable, unlike the earlier hard rubber pens, was further cause for a multitude of advertisements promoting its virtues. One outlandish ad read, "Hurled 25 Stories to Cement, Picked Up Unbroken."

Sheaffer Radites

Left to right:
a./b. *1931 pen and pencil set; Blue, Black, and White Mosaic; $200.*
c./d. *1936 Lifetime pen and pencil set, Silver and Black striped, nickel trim, $85.*
e./f. *1933 Balance Lifetime pen and pencil set, Jade, GF trim, $200.*
g. *1937 Junior, Purple and Black striped, nickel trim, $65.*
h. *1935 Burgundy and Black striped, GF trim, $55.*
i. *1932 Lifetime, Pearl and Black, GF trim, $135.*
j. *1933 Lifetime, Black and Pearl, GF trim, $135.*
k. *1934 Silver and Gray with red streaks, GF trim, $375.*
l. *1933 golf pencil, Gold Radite with Red streaks, GF trim, $60.*

Bottom:
1936 Lifetime pen and pencil, Gold Pearl Radite, GF trim, set, $235.

The Companies

Amid heavy competition to capture the fountain pen market, the "Big Four" eventually emerged: Parker, Sheaffer, Wahl, and Waterman. Theirs are the most collectible pens today (and the ones listed in this chapter). Other company names you may encounter in your collecting include the following:

Aiken Lambert	LeBoeuf
Camel	Lincoln
Carter	Moore
Chilton	Morrison
Conklin	Security
Dunn	Swan
Eclipse	Webster
Grieshaber	Weidlich
John Holland	Wirt
Laughlin	

Price Factors

Plastic pen values depend primarily on company, color, condition, and size (usually, the larger, the better). Age can also affect a pen's value, although apparently not as much as color and size. Pens are dated according to composition, shape, ink filling system, manufacturer, and color changes in a line of pens. The introduction of Parker's Black Giant and Red Giant, for instance, preceded the color revolution that began in the 1920s.

The dates listed with the photographs in this chapter are approximate. The prices reflect national prices acquired by a knowledgeable collector, and the pens are assumed to be in excellent condition unless otherwise noted.

Significant Names, Terms, and Abbreviations

Many of the pen descriptions accompanying the photographs include abbreviations, terms, and special names that may be confusing to novice collectors. The following alphabetized list should help eliminate that confusion.

Parker

a. *1918 Lucky Curve Black Giant, #12 nib, BCHR, nickel-filled trim, eyedropper filler,* **$2700–$3000.**

b. *1927 Duofold Petite Pastel, mauve-colored Permanite, GF trim, ribbon ring, button filler,* **$125.**

BCHR. Black Chased (embossed) Hard Rubber.

Early Waterman Pens

Top to bottom:

a. *1908, #52v, BCHR,* **$100.**

b. *1905 #56, BCHR, nickel clip-cap,* **$150.**

c. *1910, #20, BCHR,* **$3000 and up** (mint).

Notice how the prices go up as the pens get larger: The #20 *Waterman pictured here is a full 8½" long when open, and is very rare.*

Button filler. At the end of this pen's threaded barrel is a cap which hides a small metal "button." When the button is pushed down, the filler mechanism translates this pressure into a lateral pressure which evacuates the rubber sac beneath the barrel.

CC. Clip Cap.

Derby. Dome-shaped section at the top of the pen cap which resembles a miniature derby hat.

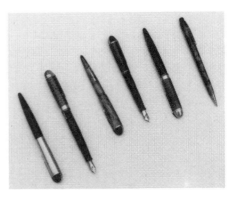

Wahl-Eversharp Pyralins, c1943

Left to right:

a. *Maroon derby, GF cap, Maroon barrel,* **$85.**

b. *GF derby, Green and Royal Blue vertical-striped cap, Royal Blue barrel, wide GF trim,* **$95.**

c. *Black derby, Silver and Black Moiré cap and barrel,* **$85.**

d. *Green derby, Green and Gold vertical-striped cap, Green barrel,* **$75.**

e. *GF derby, Maroon and Gold vertical-striped cap, Maroon barrel, wide trim band,* **$95.**

f. *Pencil, Black derby, Silver and Black Moiré,* **$80.**

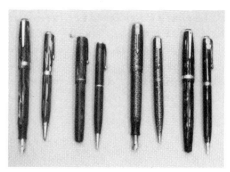

Parker Permanites

Left to right:

a./b. 1936 Duofold pen and pencil set, geometric pattern in Copper, Pearl, and
Black, GF trim, button filler, **$250.**

c./d. 1935 Duofold pen and pencil set, True
Blue (blue and white), GF trim, button
filler, **$160.**

e./f. 1934 Vacumatic pen and pencil set,
Gold and Black Web, GF trim, **$750.**

g./h. 1943 Blue Diamond Duofold pen and
pencil set, Red and Silver Pearl (with
black vertical stripes), GF trim, vacuum
filler, **$270.**

Duofold. Introduced in 1921, this line of
new, larger pens had large ink capacities
and gold points. Permanite was first used
for Duofolds in 1926.

GF. Gold Filled.

HR. Hard Rubber.

Laminated stripes. This design feature
provides a see-through barrel, allowing the
user to check the ink supply.

Loaner. A loaner pen was furnished to the
customer as a temporary replacement while
the problem pen was in the shop for repair,
since most people typically owned only one
pen.

Lucky Curve. A pen developed to pre-
vent ink from leaking out of the nib when it
is placed in a pocket. A 1913 ad described it
this way: "Now the Parker, unlike other
fountain pens, has a curved feed tube—the
famous Parker Lucky Curve. The end of it

1944–1945 Parker Permanites

Left to right:

a. Canadian Vacumatic pencil, Blue and
Black laminated stripes, GF trim, **$70.**

b. 1945 Canadian Vacumatic, Blue and
Black laminated transparent stripes, GF
trim, vacuum filler, **$125.**

c. 1945 Blue Diamond Vacumatic, Silver
and Black laminated stripes, nickel-
filled trim, **$140.**

d. 1944 Vacumatic pencil, Green and
Black laminated stripes, **$185.**

e. 1946 Blue Diamond Vacumatic, Green
and Black laminated stripes, GF trim,
vacuum filler, **$195.**

f. 1945 Blue Diamond, Black with a transparent barrel, GF trim, vacuum filler,
$85.

g./h. 1945 Blue Diamond Vacumatic pen and
pencil set, Brown and Gold laminated
transparent stripes, **$275.**

touches the barrel wall. This touch creates
capillary action, which draws all the ink
down out of the feed tube when you turn
the pen up, and before the ink expands."

Moiré. Having a wavy, vertical pattern.

Nib. The point of the pen. Point sizes are
usually indicated by a number (0–12) on the
nib. The larger the number, the larger the
nib. Sometimes there can be other indica-
tions, as with Waterman's No. 7, where
there is a colored band or dot on the top of
the cap.

Waterman Patricians (Pyralin)

Left: *1934, Onyx, GF trim,* **$1200.**

Top to bottom, center:
a.   *1933, Jet Black, no cap, GF trim,* **$1250 and up.**
b./c. *1929 pen and pencil set, Nacre (black and pearl), chromium trim,* **set, $1500.**

Right: *1930, Turquoise, GF trim,* **$1500.**

Waterman

Left to right:
a./b. *1935, #84-S, Silver Ray, chrome-plated trim, ray filler; pen, pencil,* **$195.**
c.   *1934 Lady Patricia, Red Lace pattern, ray filler,* **$135.**
d.   *1935, #84-S, Silvery Green Ray, ray filler,* **$475.**
e.   *1935 Lady Patricia, Silver Lace pattern, ray filler,* **$125.**

Patrician. The Patrician, called a *prestige pen,* was advertised as "the very finest and most beautiful fountain pen for men." Typically, it is a large fountain pen characterized by an oversized point. Even in the 1920s, a Patrician cost $10.

The **Lady Patricia** was advertised as an attractive accessory for a lady's handbag, a pen with "many features dear to the feminine heart—dainty jewel-like design—slender grip—and a chic modern clasp [to hold it upright in a handbag]."

Streamlined. Tapered.

Parker Streamlined Permanites

Left to right:
a. *1929 Duofold De Luxe pencil, Moderne Black and Pearl, GF trim,* **$250.**
b. *1931 Duofold Sr., Black, GF trim, button filler,* **$425.**
c. *1931 Duofold Sr., Jade, GF trim, button filler,* **$425.**
d. *1930 Duofold Jr., Mandarin Yellow, GF trim, button filler,* **$300.**
e. *1929 Duofold pencil, Mandarin Yellow, GF trim, ribbon ring,* **$165.**
f. *1929 Duofold pen, Naples Blue, GF trim, ribbon ring, button filler,* **$200.**
g. *1932 Duofold Sr., Burgundy and Black, GF trim, button filler,* **$475.**

Bottom:
1931 Duofold Jr. pencil, Jade, GF trim, **$90.**

109

13
Other Items from the Office or Study

Forest green Celluloid desk set with cream trim; includes a letter holder, perpetual calendar, blotter, box, and pen holder, **set, $85.**

This chapter includes several groups of items that are usually collected by specific category instead of together. What most have in common is their place in or on the desk: calendars, pen and pencil holders, letter openers, paperweights, bookends, rulers, cigarette boxes, ashtrays, and so on.

You will find a wide range of quality—and thus, of prices—in these categories. Some of these objects sound fairly common, but as usual, any unique twist tends to make them more collectible, and rarity increases their value.

Celluloid bookmark with perpetual calendar fabric insert and flower design hand-painted in oils, **$20.**

*"Puffed" Celluloid notepad, cream, **$20**.*

*Double inkwell in brown Bakelite with porce-lain inserts, Fabrication Française, France, **$60**.*

*Bakelite magnifying glass with woodpecker, **$100**.*

*Souvenir bookmark (Celluloid) with hand-painted logo from the University of Marburg in Germany, nineteenth century, **$25**.*

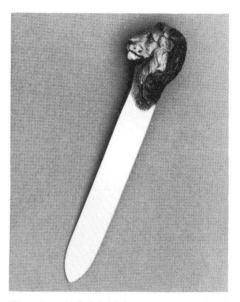

*Lion-shaped Celluloid letter opener, painted details, **$67**.*

In General

From the early twentieth century, collect-ibles include Bakelite bookends, pen hold-ers, and paperweights. Celluloid objects more often include rulers, pens and pen-cils, letter openers, and book page slicers (librarians and booksellers often had to slice book pages apart themselves). Early books sometimes have Celluloid covers, and there are even some Celluloid calen-dars and small notebooks on the antiques market. In all these plastics, look for the Art Deco lines typical of the times.

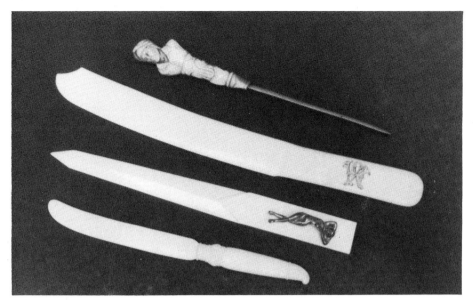

Top to bottom:

a. *Figural Celluloid letter opener,* **$65.**
b. *Monogrammed Celluloid page slicer,* **$50.**
c. *Double-edged letter Celluloid letter opener with metal nude mount,* **$90.**
d. *Celluloid letter opener with decorative handle,* **$25.**

Handmade Lucite (acrylic) letter opener with leather case, $15.

Black Bakelite pen holder with Art Deco hexagon decoration and Catalin "tortoiseshell" pen top, **$35.**

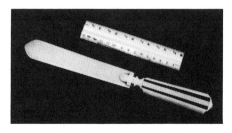

Celluloid ruler, 6" long, **$10.** *Nineteenth-century page slicer of ivory and black Celluloid,* **$35.** **Rare.**

113

Mile-O-Graph mileage measurer by Mile-O-Graph, Inc., New York, $5.

Paragon Autograph Album, embossed Celluloid front cover, dark turquoise velvet-covered binder, nineteenth century, $25.

Top: *Nineteenth-century Celluloid photograph album with birds embossed on cover, 1895, $60.* **Rare.** From the collection of Vera Leister, Westminster, MD.

Bottom: *Interior view of photograph album; note the hand-lettered title page, done in a style known as* flourishing.

Later collectible objects in this category are typically 1940s, 1950s, and 1960s hard plastics such as polystyrene. Marbleized plastics are already showing up at respected markets, along with advertising rulers, paperweights, and other articles.

Book of poetry (Lowell's Poems) *in Celluloid cover tied with bow, $25.* From the collection of the Carroll County Farm Museum, Westminster, MD.

Desktop pen holder, green and gold marble-ized Bakelite with metal elephant decoration, **$65.**

Marbleized purple pencil/pen holder on revolving metal base, **$45.** *From the author's collection.*

Marbleized taupe pencil box, **$20.**

Red Midget pencil sharpener, Apsco Products, Inc., Los Angeles, CA, **$10.**

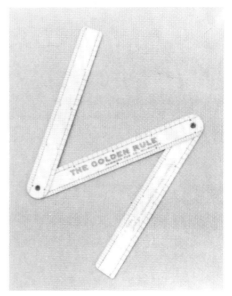

Celluloid folding ruler, marked The Golden Rule, Hammond Pub. Co., Milwaukee, **$15.**

Tobacco-Related Items

Smoking was in its heyday from the first part of this century through the 1950s. As a result, an extensive amount of smoking paraphernalia from this period is available to the collector today. Some of these objects are rarely made or used in connection with smoking anymore.

Bakelite cigar holder with its original case, marked C.P.F., *$50.*

Dice lighters: butterscotch Bakelite with black dots, and black and white dots, **each, $60.**

Top: *Cigarette holder in tortoiseshell, ivory, and black Bakelite, $28.*

Also shown:
a. *Scottie pencil sharpener, red Bakelite, $25.*
b. *Red and black Bakelite pencil, $15.*
c. *Lime green Bakelite pen, $18.*
d. *Yellow and green mechanical pencil, $20.*
e. *Black and marbleized green pen, $15.*

Not pictured: *Pink, blue, and yellow windmill pencil holder with dog (in original box), Celluloid, marked* Occupied Japan, *2½" high, $35.*

Acrylic layered lighter; white, black, and red layers; $95.

At one time, for example, it was common to have a special container for cigarettes on your desk or coffee table. Now these cigarette boxes have truly become a part of history. Because of this—and because of their beauty, style, design, and usefulness as cache boxes—they are highly collectible today.

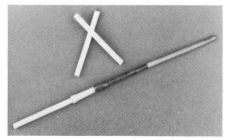

Celluloid "movie star" cigarette holder made in three sections: red, marbleized red, and white, $30.

Brown Bakelite smoker's set with gold- and silver-colored metal decorations, Brown and Bigelow, St. Paul, MN, **set, $35.**

Bakelite smoker's set containing ashtray, cigarette case, and a place for matches, **$45.**

Gutta Percha match safe embossed with a maltese cross and marked Baker Fabric Firehose, The Gutta Percha and Rubber Mfg. Co., NY, **$95. Rare.** From the collection of Beverly Smith, Sykesville, MD.

Acrylic cigarette box (made by my father-in-law), 1950s, **$45.**

Black Bakelite cigarette box with embossed buck and doe decoration, **$45.**

Beetleware cigarette box, cream Celluloid with embossed bird decoration on the lid, made for the Centennial Celebration of the American Patent System, **$60.**

Black, green, and yellow marbleized cigarette box, Catalin Corp., NY, **$95.**

Urea cigarette box with embossed figure on pierced lid, black bottom, $25.

These cigarette boxes often appear in Lucite, Bakelite, and more contemporary plastics. The Art Deco boxes are of special interest to collectors at present because of the style's recent revival. If Deco boxes are of extremely good quality and style, they bring even more money. Look for racing horses, borzois, airplanes, and chrome accents. Also remember chrome items with Bakelite accents, such as the expensive and highly desirable Chase pieces.

Red and black Bakelite cigarette box with Art Deco horse motif, $28. Brown Bakelite ashtray by the GES Line, probably used in a restaurant or other commercial establishment, common, $6. Green and brown marbleized pen knife, $20.

Art Deco cigarette box (Bakelite): When the top button is pushed, a door opens on each of its six sides to reveal a cache of cigarettes. It also has a Swiss music box that plays "Star Dust" and "Two Cigarettes in the Dark," $65.

Black Bakelite cigarette box with Art Deco lines; on the lid, metal medallion shows a horseman; 3" × 4"; $28.

Marbleized Bakelite cigarette box with chrome lid and base; the cigarettes come out when the lid is raised, $95.

Good Prospects

Office and study collectibles of immediate future interest to collectors include bright-colored hard plastics, novelty and souvenir paperweights (especially those that might be classified as art objects in themselves), and objects such as staplers that have become outdated in comparison to more contemporary models.

119

Part Three

JUST

FOR

FUN

Bright orange Disney Pluto, jointed, Dakin, 8″ long, **$27.**

14

Celebrity and Character Toys

Of all the plastic toys that have enjoyed success as collectibles, those which are in some way related to celebrities (such as athletes and media personalities) or cartoon characters tend to be the most valuable. Because of their special value, these items occupy a chapter of their own; keep in mind that they could be crossovers. Chapter 18 describes some of the same kinds of toys included here, while this chapter focuses solely on their classification as famous people/character toys.

Beatles

Some of the most expensive toys in this area of collecting are the Beatles items. In fact, you will see unreasonably high prices for Beatles collectibles, and you will have to decide for yourself whether the investment is worth it. I bought the set of nodding Beatles pictured here seven years ago for $9, and people thought I had lost my mind. Now, as the description indicates, the set is worth $185.

Brown vinyl Woodsy Owl, anti-pollution promotional toy, Dakin, **$25.**

Beatles nodders, Hong Kong, 3¹/₂" tall, **set of 4, $185.**

Ringo Starr bubble bath container, made by NEMS Enterprises, LTD, for the Colgate-Palmolive Corp., NY, 1965, **$125.**

Cartoon Characters

The cartoon character dolls pictured in this chapter are very highly sought after. They have good detail, they are jointed, and they have well-made clothing that is actually cloth. Most of them originally came in plastic bags with paper labels tied to them. Be alert for these MIB (Mint—In Box) items.

Barney Rubble and Fred Flintstone, marked Hanna-Barbara Prod., *vinyl with cloth clothing,* Dakin, 1970, **each, $30.**

Mickey Mouse dressed as a cowboy, Durham Industries, NY, **$45.**

Beatles New Sound guitar, marked Selcol, Made in England under licence, *1960s,* **$185.**

Mickey Mouse figures showing the difference between the older, more collectible toy (left) and the newer one: original Mickey Mouse, Louis Marx and Co., USA, 1971, 5½" tall, $20; the other toy, made in Hong Kong, has painted eyes that are focused differently, $10.

Dakin. Dakin, which began making its toys in 1957, may be the next Steiff of toy collecting. Although most of Dakin's better-known products are cloth or felt stuffed toys, the company's plastics are already rising in value, with some of the most valuable being the cartoon character ones made of vinyl.

When you're considering a Dakin purchase, be sure that all the clothing is on the doll or toy, that all the parts are still intact, and that no parts are chewed or broken off. Usually, ink or crayon marks are not removable, and dirty clothing can only be cleaned with difficulty, if at all.

Porky Pig and Elmer Fudd, jointed vinyl, Dakin, **each, $45.**

Olive Oyl (from the Popeye cartoon), vinyl, Dakin, 1960s, $65. **Rare.**

Pez containers. For years, toy dealers have offered Pez candy containers as additions to specialty collections. Now they are a crossover collectible; Disney collectors, cartoon collectors, and Pez collectors alike will want the Disney series, for example. Despite such demand, prices for these containers are still low, but they're going up at shows. Expect to pay 25¢ (or less) each at a yard sale, $1.00 at a flea market, and $5–$100 at an antiques show. However, if you find a rare one you don't have at a higher price, just remember this rule of thumb for collectors: Buy it when you see it, or someone else will.

For more information on collecting Pez containers, see Chapter 18.

Pez Candy Containers

Left to right:
a. *Porky Pig, Austria,* **$20.**
b. *Batman, D.C. Comics, USA, 1978,* **$30.**
c. *The Joker (from the Batman comics), D.C. Comics, USA, 1978,* **$65. Rare.**
d. *The Hulk, Marvel Group, Hong Kong, 1978,* **$6.**
e. *Disney's Scrooge McDuck, Hong Kong (make sure he still has his spectacles),* **$10.**
f. *Disney's Pluto, attached ears, Austria,* **$3–$5.**
g. *Mickey Mouse, Yugoslavia or Hong Kong (make sure his nose is still intact), common,* **$3–$5.**

Other TV and Movie-Related Items

Even recent toys (Star Wars items, for instance) in this category command good prices. The Star Trek doll pictured in this chapter is just one of many such items by Mego. Hartland toys (see the Rin Tin Tin and the Roy Rogers and Trigger photographs) are now very expensive. Keep a sharp watch for them.

Not pictured: *Baltimore Colts football player, Hartland,* **$180.** *Also look for the bowler,* **$75,** *and a 4" tall batter,* **$125.**

Hartland Rin Tin Tin, marked on the inside of one rear leg, common, **$35.** From the author's collection.

Hartland Roy Rogers and Trigger (hat and gun missing), **$125;** *Dale Evans,* **$110.**

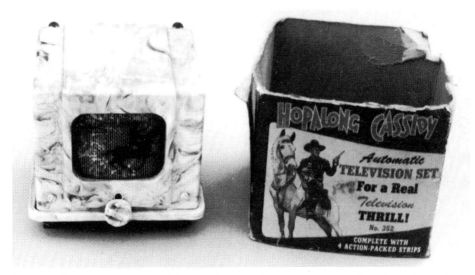

Hopalong Cassidy automatic television set, Automatic Toy Co., Staten Island, NY, early 1950s, **$95.**

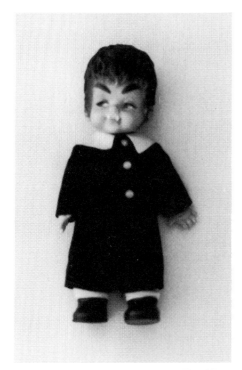

Eddie (the son in the TV show, "The Munsters"), marked Ideal Toy Corp., *Japan, 1965,* **$40. Rare.**

Look for Captain Kirk, Dr. McCoy, Mr. Spock, and Lt. Uhura in Star Trek dolls such as this 8" tall version by Mego; **each, $40–$65.**

The Hulk, green, jointed, $15.

Mickey Mouse, jointed, Dakin, $40.

Price Factors

In general, items in a series are more collectible than those that are not. A very rare individual item, however, could be priced higher than an entire series if the series is fairly common.

Pez collectibles. On Disney containers, look for the *Walt Disney Production* name in tiny letters on the head. These are better than the unmarked Mickey Mouse containers pictured in this chapter. In addition, you will find *DC Comics* marked on the Batman items, and *Marvel* on many other cartoon or comic characters. Dates are sometimes listed, too.

Also keep in mind that a patent date is just that; the item could actually have been made years later. In any case, collectors prefer marked and dated items.

Vinyl Minnie Mouse, Dakin, $45.

Batman barrette, mint, **$18,** *and Batman compass (on a wristband), mint,* **$30;** *NEMO, National Periodical Pub., Inc., 1966.*

Good Prospects

It is likely that currently made cartoon, character, and series items will eventually be as collectible as the older ones pictured, as is suggested by the popularity of toys as recent as the Darth Vader included here.

Darth Vader, Star Wars figure from The Empire Strikes Back, *15" tall,* **$35.** *Be sure he still has his original cape and sword.*

15

Dolls and Doll Furniture

Because doll collecting is such an extensive, established field, this chapter does not attempt to cover all its aspects. Rather, it includes a sampling of some of the high prices now offered for plastic dolls, and it discusses some of the peculiarities of those dolls. In addition, part of the chapter is devoted to Renwal doll furniture, the finest available in plastic.

Teen Fashions Jill doll (in original box), hard plastic, Vogue, 1950s, 9³/₄″ tall, $100; $75 without box.

Shirley Temple doll in a Heidi costume, hard plastic and vinyl, Ideal Toy Corp., c1957, 12″ tall, $150.

131

Binnie toddler, hard plastic and vinyl, plaid dress, Madame Alexander, c1964, 18" tall, $335. From the collection of Beverly Smith, Sykesville, MD

Miss Curity, original nurse uniform, P-90 hard plastic, Ideal Toy Corp., $225. From the collection of Beverly Smith, Sykesville, MD.

The Celluloids

Since its invention, Celluloid has been used to make all types of dolls. Many of the early ones had glass eyes, some had kid bodies, and many were twins of bisques produced at the same time. Some early German Celluloids had a turtle mark, along with the word *Schutzmarke* (German for *trademark*). Earlier dolls were usually made out of a heavier substance than was used for the later, Made-in-Japan variety, which tended to be very thin and were often decorated with feathers or sequins (such as the Kewpie carnival prizes).

Mechanicals. Celluloid mechanical dolls and toys also became popular in the early 1900s; see the wind-up, crawling version in this chapter. Also available are acrobats and even swimmers—the ones that didn't wind up made great bath toys.

Celluloid mechanicals are crossover items which are prized by toy collectors as well as by plastic collectors.

Problems. Celluloid dolls have a number of composition problems. Because they were flammable and fragile, they did not last long, so there are not that many

P-90 hard plastic doll issued to promote Toni home permanents, original light green dress and patent leather shoes, Ideal Toy Corp., c1949, 14" tall, $130.

Wind-up Celluloid with cloth outfit, $35. (If marked Occupied Japan, a similar doll sells for $75.

Ginger, Girl Scout uniform, Cosmopolitan, 8" tall, mint, $85.

around. In those you do find, look for cracks and dents. Plus, restringing is nearly impossible for these dolls. Avoid those with detached limbs.

Another problem with some of the first Celluloids—especially in comparison to the bisques—was their unnatural glossy look. Some companies got rid of the gloss by rubbing their dolls with a pumice stone or powder. Also in an attempt to correct the gloss situation, William Carpenter received a patent in 1880 for improving Celluloid dolls.

Finally, these dolls tended to fade in sunlight. The pink Celluloid faded more readily than the black dolls, so black dolls are usually in better condition.

Special finds. Dolls made in Occupied Japan, marked when the United States occupied Japan after World War II, are always worth more. Wind-ups sell for $35–$45, and plain ones are $25–$30.

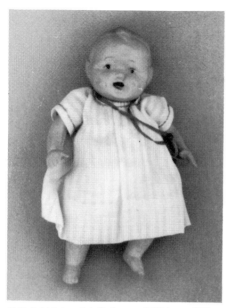

Celluloid jointed doll, Japan, 6½" long, $25.

Kissing Celluloids had magnets in their lips. Bride and groom versions are worth the most ($20–$25 a pair) because they are so widely collected.

Modern Dolls

According to *The History of Dolls,* by Constance King, the first modern plastic dolls were made by Riedeler, of the German Democratic Republic, in 1948. Since then, an unlimited variety of dolls have been sold, from Barbie to The Incredible Hulk. See the preceding chapter for more of the highly desirable cartoon character and celebrity dolls.

Celluloid doll with jointed arms and painted pink dress, 6" tall, $28.

Pammi, part vinyl, wearing original polyester clothes and hat; this doll could only be purchased on the Auto Train. Effanbee, 1966, 14" tall, $200. Rare.

Doll wearing handmade dress, 7" tall, $12.

Rub-A-Dub doll, Ideal Toy Corp., 1973, $35; white version, $22. From the collection of Evelyn Moore, Westminster, MD.

Renwal Doll Furniture

Renwal dollhouse furniture was produced between the 1940s and the 1960s. Although it was considered a cheap imitation of the finer wooden furniture when it was first produced, it is now considered a quality collector's item by dollhouse enthusiasts.

Robert Hencey writes of Renwal dollhouse furniture (*Rarities*, May/June 1983), "In 1948, for example, anyone's daughter could furnish a six-room playtime mansion with 49 Renwal pieces for the magnificent sum of $6.75." Pieces could be purchased by room sets as well. Today, each piece costs $5 and up, on the average, depending upon rarity, condition, and date of manufacture. Older washing machines and sewing machines are in the $20 range, for instance, and smaller objects such as lamps are $5-$10. Earlier pieces may have an even higher value because of their detail: An early stove may have a working door, for instance, while the later model does not.

Although other companies such as Superior, Acme, Ideal, and Mar have produced plastic dollhouse furniture, their products do not have the durability or fine quality and detail of the Renwal pieces. Much of the Renwal furniture has movable parts. Drawers on dressers open, doors on refrigerators open, the shelves are removable, and legs and arms on the tiny dolls are jointed. (I even had a set of folding card-table chairs when I was a child.) The pieces shown in this chapter are black, but the furniture was made in many other colors.

Details of Renwal furniture are authentic, right down to patterns embossed on sofas to look like cloth upholstery, and a moving treadle sewing machine. Many of the pieces are identical (though miniature) copies of the originals of the period. This makes it especially interesting to study the tiny appliances, to note the revival of Federal furniture, and to see the accessories used, such as pedestal ashtrays.

*Dollhouse rocker with hand-painted flowers and chairs with decals, Product No. 65, Renwal, common, **each, $12**.*

Good Prospects

It appears that Renwal furniture will continue to lead the plastic doll furniture market, but since many people are unaware of its value, there are still a lot of good buys available.

With so many doll collectors around, almost any dolls seem to become collectible as soon as they hit the market, but if you have a strong interest in this area, consult some up-to-date resources for specific information. The *Wallace-Homestead Price Guide to Dolls* contains several lists—of major doll publications, antique and collectible publications, and North American doll and toy museums—to which you might want to refer.

16

Games

Perhaps it's difficult for you to imagine that plastic game pieces are actually collectible. After all, they seem so new in comparison to many of the games they're used in, which are thousands of years old. They have, however, been in use longer than you might think. Even as far back as the late nineteenth century, Celluloid was used for game pieces to replace the already-rare (and expensive) ivory.

Mah-jongg set with Bakelite playing pieces, **$150.**

In addition to these classics, more recently popular (and often, forgotten) games made use of plastic playing pieces. Many of them are puzzles, such as the ones pictured here.

Double Master Set of Hi-Q, Tryne Sales, Inc., NY, 1960s, **$10.**

On Me game block, Bakelite, marked Made exclusively for the House of Gadgets, Inc., New York, USA, **$38.**

*The Fisherman Puzzle and The Sailboat Puzzle, J. W. Dreuke, 1948, **each, $20.***

*31 Puzzle with original box; moving the numbered squares into certain patterns was similar to working the more recent puzzle, Rubik's Cube; **$15.***

*Majestic card shuffler, brown Bakelite, **$25.***

*Purple-red marbleized card holder, NuDell Plastic, Chicago, IL, **$18.***

Cards

Card playing, once thought to be the work of the devil, had become acceptable by the turn of the century, which opened up the market for card-related items. Card holders and card boxes—whether Bakelite, Celluloid, or more recent types of plastic—are quite popular collectibles. Besides having ornamental value, the ones with closed lids can also serve as caché boxes.

*Red, white, and blue urea poker chips with jockey motif, **set of 200 (approximately), $40.***

Set of red, yellow, white, and blue poker chips in a marbleized taupe-colored box, $20.

Marbleized green Catalin dice cup and red-dotted ivory dice, AP Games, $35.

Left: *Bridge Tally Score Keeper, marbleized green Celluloid, $20.* Also pictured: *matching address book, marked* Souvenir of Atlantic City, *$15, and engagement book, $15.*

Cribbage. One of the earliest card games was cribbage. The surface of a cribbage board contains holes where pegs are to be placed (to represent the score of the game). The pegs are often stored in a hidden compartment in the board. Make sure the pegs are there and that the door on the compartment is not lost. In the case of acrylic boards, make sure there are no scratches.

Consider adding a cribbage board or two to your collection. They are rarer than most game sets, and may eventually attract as much attention as the well-known game boards.

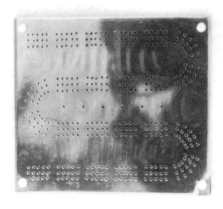

Acrylic cribbage board (made by my father in the 1950s), 9″ × 10″, $50.

Chess

Early, expensive chess sets were often made of wood, bone, ivory, silver or other metals, or ceramic. Since the advent of plastics, sets have become much more accessible to the masses, and with the rising number manufactured, the variety of shapes among the game pieces has also increased. Now there are even sets in the shape of astronauts or of vegetables; look for unusual pieces such as these.

Composition chess board with painted green and white squares and contrasting red and white plastic men, 1950s, $30.

Make sure the sets are complete as follows: one king, one queen, two bishops, two knights, two castles, and eight pawns for each side, for a total of 32 pieces. Collectors should also beware of sets that do not match. In most cases, single pieces are not as valuable, but they may be worth buying, especially if they are early. Later plastic sets are more likely to be complete, so individual pieces from these, or broken sets, may be of little value.

Dominoes

For years dominoes were virtually unnoticed unless they were ivory. Now collectors want Celluloid, Bakelite, and other plastic sets, especially those which have advertisements or come in their original boxes. Lately, in fact, game collectors have been silently sweeping the best domino games right off the market.

Domino sets should also be complete, with a double-6 set having 28 pieces and a double-9 set having 56.

A size comparison: BG Dominos (new), made in France, $30, and miniature dominoes (with an L embossed on each) in their original box, Lowe Co., Inc., NY, $35.

Heavy, black and white dominoes, Bakelite, in original, dove-tailed box; each domino is held together by a metal screw, $65.

*Celluloid dominoes with painted red dots, **set**, $68.*

Good Prospects

Already, computer (and other types of electronically played) games are becoming collectible. Both the game units and the cartridges in these are made primarily of plastic.

Combat!, green case with camouflage label, Coleco Industries, Inc., Amsterdam, NY, $20. From the author's collection.

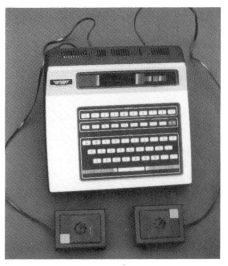

Magnavox's Odyssey Z, North American Phillips Consumer Electronics Corp., 1981, $20. Tapes: Bowling, Basketball, Spinout, The Quest of the Rings, UFO; each, $6. Children's tapes, such as Math-A-Magic, sell for less; each, $3. From the author's collection.

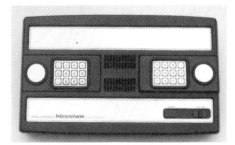

Intellivision, Model 2609, Mattel Electronics, Hawthorne, CA, $25; tapes, each, $8. From the author's collection.

TV Fun (plays tennis and hockey only), APF Electronics, Inc., Japan, $20. From the author's collection.

17

Models/Cars

Models

There are two types of model collectors: One collects models that have never been built and are still in their original boxes, and the other collects models that have been partially or completely assembled. Examples from each category have been included in this chapter.

Platform railway power station with great detail, Vollmer, W. Germany, $35.

MIB (Mint—In Box)

An item of this type is priced according to its rarity, the manufacturer, and the condition of the box. Collecting fields include automobiles, space-related objects, science fiction objects, comic and cartoon characters, TV- and movie-related objects, ships and airplanes (especially war models),

Brick-look train-yard building, Vollmer, W. Germany, $45.

scenes and series, and miscellaneous models such as dinosaurs and the Visible Dog, which is pictured on the following page.

Built Models

In general, assembled models do not command the prices that the MIB models do, but there are still plenty of interested buyers who usually pay somewhere in the $10–$20 range for one of them.

Visible Dog, 1960s, $45.

Left to right:
a. *Yellow car with white wheels, Auburn Rubber, 3¾" long, $25.*
b. *Brown car with white wheels, USA, 4" long, $25.*
c. *Green WWII Army truck, rubber tires, Thomas, 3½" long, $30.*

Procter and Gamble give-aways: At left, Fun-mate, orange Ford Torino without propeller (deleted because propellers were judged unsafe for children), $20. Earlier model, yellow Go-Car with propeller, Japan, $28.

Cars. American automobiles are a favorite in this category. If the prices are fair, these models usually disappear only an hour or two after they have been offered for sale. There seem to be even fewer foreign car models available, especially older ones, since the foreign car market has not always been as big in the United States as it is now.

Many of the collectibles pictured in this chapter were given away by dealers to promote a new line of automobiles. These often list dealer specifications for the model year on the bottom. As you might expect, the more popular the actual car, the more popular its collectible model.

1962 promo, Chevrolet Impala convertible, unpainted white plastic, specifications on bottom, $200.

1961 promo, Ford Galaxie 500, two-door, hardtop, painted gray, car specifications on bottom, $75.

1968–69 promo (left), Ford Maverick, gold, $25. 1979 promo, red Corvette, $35.

1968 promo (left), Lincoln Continental, red, $55. 1980 promo, yellow Corvette, $35.

1962 promo (left), Plymouth Fury, beige, Jo-Han Models, Detroit, MI, $40. 1966 promo, Thunderbird, red, $85.

Other vehicles. Ships, planes, and space vehicles are also in demand, especially those from popular shows. Some of the most desirable right now are the Star Trek models by AMT, the last of which were issued in 1977. Look for more recent versions to be good investments—the A-Team van and Star Wars models, for example.

Celebrity/character kits. As with other toys, there is quite a market for models dealing with celebrities and cartoon, TV, and movie characters: Note the 1960s Revell kit featuring Ringo Starr of the Beatles, which sells for $185 constructed. Many of these are also collected, either built or not, by fans who are not normally collectors.

Handmade models. Though they are rare, there are some handmade models which are highly collectible. Most are acrylic, and many are art objects like Robert the Robot (see the color section).

You will also see customized versions of purchased kits, which are collected by those who prefer constructed models. The more interesting and the higher the quality of these custom models, the more they are worth.

Condition. The condition of already-constructed models is not as important as that of MIB objects. Occasionally, a piece or two can be missing from a desirable car and a collector will still want it. Still, try to find any object in the best condition possible, because the perfect one will always be more desirable and have a higher value.

When assessing condition, look for a well-painted model without glue drips. If the model is a snap-together (instead of glued) version, check loose-feeling pieces to be sure that nothing has been broken. Remember, these were amateur projects, and the quality of assembly varies.

Cereal give-aways from the 1950s and 1960s, F. & F. Mold and Die Works, Dayton, OH, **each, $8–$25.** *The police car is the rarest; $25.*

1964 Thunderbird (left), mustard, **$125.** *1964 Rambler Classic, white with gray painted roof,* **$30.**

1969 promo (left), *Galaxie Sunliner, white convertible, AMT, Birmingham, MI,* **$75.** *1965 promo, Mustang Fastback, red,* **$175.**

Model Manufacturers

Look for the following trademarks in your collecting:

Addams	Italeri
Addar	ITC
Advent	Lifelike
Airfix	Lindberg
AMT	Mikro
Aurora	Monogram
Bachman	MPC
Convair	M. Shokai & Co.,
Entex	Japan
Faller	Precision
Frog	Pyro
Games Science Corp.	Renwal
Hartland	Revell
Hawk	Strombecker
	Unimog

Good Prospects

Here are a few ideas for kits you might want to consider as investments:

- *Currently popular car models.* These will undoubtedly hold just as much fascination for future generations as 1950s Thunderbirds hold for so many today.
- *High-quality kits.* Although these are almost always more expensive with the original purchase, they should fare extra well as future collectibles because there are normally fewer sold if the kit is more expensive.

- *Historical items.* Space-related models, as indicated above, are already being collected; such vehicles as the space shuttle certainly mark a significant time in history. Similar historically representative vehicles should also make good buys.
- *Science fiction.* Japanese models in this category are best, but there will be collectors for American versions, too.
- *Series.* Series have always been popular in the collecting world, especially those that have limited runs and are discontinued after a period of time.

White 1957 Thunderbird, promo, **$200;** *kit,* **$10.**

Plum 1934 Mercedes Benz 540, **$10.**

Additional Prices

Note: Most items are indicated as built or boxed.

Addar

a. Blue Jays in a bottle, boxed, **$15.**
b. Evel Knievel and Skycycle, boxed, **$20.**
c. *Planet of the Apes* characters, boxed, **each, $20.**

Airfix

a. Henry VIII, boxed, **$15.**
b. Joan of Arc, boxed, **$25.**
c. #2-88 BAC 1-11 Mohawk, boxed, **$25.**

AMT

a. Enterprise, electronic, original large box, **$200-$295.**
b. Klingon, earlier version (1976), **$125.**
c. Mr. Spock, from *Star Trek: The Motion Picture,* 6″ tall, built, **$30.**

Aurora

a. Comic scenes: Superman, Batman, Tarzan, Tonto, boxed, **each, $65.** Lone Ranger, built, **$40.**
b. Bachman, Bassett Hound, boxed, **$25.**
c. Dr. Jekyll and Mr. Hyde, snap model, boxed, **$75.**
d. Lindberg, Glow UFO, reissue, **$40.**

MPS

a. Disney's Escape from the Crypt, **$50.**
b. Strange Change Time Machine, box, **$30.**
c. Strange Change Vampire, **$30.**
d. Strange Change Mummy, **$30.**

Boeing B-47 labeled Giant Stratojet Bomber, *H 206:98, Revell (unassembled is worth more), $15 each.* Same price, not pictured: *H-307 Aircraft Carrier, H-302 Chris Craft, H-212 Grumman Cougar, H-415 1849 Flying Cloud, H-210 Lockhead F940.*

Revell

a. Brother Rat Fink, boxed, **$20.**
b. Cat in the Hat, boxed, **$25.**
c. Eastern Connie, H245, 5″, boxed, **$40.**
d. Endangered Rhino, boxed, **$20.**
e. Condor, boxed, **$20.**
f. Ratfink in Lotus slot car, boxed, **$35.**
g. Ringo Starr, built, **$185.**

Strombecker

a. #D31 PAAA China Clipper, **$75.**
b. Lunar Reconnaissance Vehicle, boxed, **$45.**
c. Nuclear Interplanetary Vehicle, boxed, **$45.**

Cars

In the category of adult toys, a number of plastic-bodied cars are becoming collectible—see the Corvette pictured. Look, too, for original Avantis, which are even higher priced, and other examples such as Saab Sonnet and Daimler sports cars.

1972 Chevrolet Corvette Stingray coupe with removable, T-top panels, a continuation of the 1968 design inspired by the Mako Shark II show car. Fiberglass body over steel chassis. Early models are most desirable, $8,000–$10,000 (in excellent condition). From the collection of JoAnn Hunter, Manchester, MD.

18

Miscellaneous Toys

Modern plastics were a boon to the toy industry. With their invention, parents could finally choose safer, less expensive, and eventually, nonflammable and unbreakable toys for their children. Now, toy collectors are seeing an interesting variety of plastic items which have survived, basically, because of the very qualities that brought them favor with their original buyers.

Baby-Related

Because of the heavy abuse baby-related toys usually get, few of the early ones remain today, especially the Celluloid ones. Of all the plastic toys produced, Celluloids were probably the most fragile, cracking and denting easily. Since they had the extra disadvantage of being flammable, it is surprising any survived at all. Still, Celluloid dolls, rattles, and outdoor animals (used for Christmas decorations) were produced well into the early twentieth century, and some of these items are now part of the collectibles market. Study Celluloids carefully before you buy them to be sure that they have no hidden cracks, which lower value.

Clown roly-poly, bright orange and yellow, 1940s or 1950s, **$35.**

Crib toy; black, butterscotch, and olive green, **$125. Rare.**

151

Top: *Goose nodder, marked* S. A. Reider, *NYC, Germany, 3" long,* **$28;** *four Celluloid fish, 1½" long,* **each, $12. Rare.**

Bottom: *Celluloid dog, 3" long,* **$18.** *Celluloid hippo, 4" long,* **$20.**

Early 1900s Celluloid baby articles: Pacifier, **$28,** *and clown rattle,* **$48.**

Top: *Celluloid man, 2½" tall,* **$18;** *rattle with face design,* **$15** *(if complete—the handle is missing from the one pictured).*

Bottom: *Celluloid horse, 4½" long,* **$22.** *Celluloid rattle, 2½" high,* **$36.**

Celluloid roly-polies, **each, $68.**

Even more rare are the Bakelite rattles and crib toys. Of the few produced, many fell apart because the pieces were so heavy. Despite their rarity, these turn-of-the-century toys seem to be priced rather low at the moment, which should make them reasonable investments.

Baby toys from the 1940s and 1950s are also becoming collectible, particularly rubber ones from Auburn. Rubber deteriorates rapidly, so be careful when checking the condition of these. Also keep in mind that rubber, like Celluloid, should be protected from high temperatures (see Appendix A).

Battery-Operated

There are still a lot of good battery toys (such as the Action Jackson series) on the market. The ones from the 1950s and early 1960s are most often metal, but a few good buys in plastic from the 1950s through the 1970s do exist.

Battery toys are priced by the number of actions they perform. The more actions, the higher a toy's price, considering that other criteria such as condition and quality have already passed inspection. Beware of rotted rubber parts and leaky battery boxes.

Wild Mustang battery toy from Mego's Action Jackson Double Action series, original box, brown and beige, Hong Kong, 1971, 8" high, **$45.** *The tail moves as the horse walks.* Not pictured (each available at price of Wild Mustang): *Action Jackson Rescue Copter, Scramble Cycle, Snowmobile, Jumping Jeep, Strap-On Helicopter, Water Scooter, and Fire Rescue Pack.*

Sheep crib toy; white, butterscotch, ivory, and light blue Bakelite, **$35.**

Battery-powered Flasher, red, Electric Animals, Inc., NY, 5¼" high, **$25.**

Pelican battery toy, day-glo pink plastic covered with fake fur, **$28.**

*Toucan battery toy, 24" high, **$165**.*

Watch for battery toys marked *Made in USA*, as well as those marked *Japan* or *Hong Kong*. (The ones made in China are much newer.) They're usually better buys and will continue to go up in value.

Figures

Collectors are beginning to take a serious look at all kinds of plastic figures, and there is great diversity in this area. For example, celebrity figures and cartoon characters such as The Hulk, Mickey Mouse, and Porky Pig (see Chapter 14) are desirable, as well as warriors, cowboys, and soldiers (which could go up in value, even appearing with lead soldiers and Britains in some collections). Then there are the comic figures pictured in this chapter, and so on.

*100 Toy Soldiers (ranging from one to four inches long), original box, green, Carle Place, L.I., NY, **set**, **$25**.* From the collection of Audrey Meyer, Sykesville, MD.

Nutty Mads—Each is about 6" tall; most are green or lavender.

Left to right:
*a. Waldo, **$10**.*
*b. Manny the Reckless Mariner, **$10**.*
*c. End Zone, **$15**.*
From the author's collection.

*Protester doll, vinyl with fake fur hair, 1960s, 5" tall, **$12**.*

As with other collectibles, sets and series of plastic figures are usually worth more than individual pieces. However, if collectors are competing for a rare figure to complete a set that has otherwise been easy to assemble, the price of that one figure may suddenly rise a good bit.

*Tiny 12, set of translucent figures in original box, including swan, squirrel, horse, dog, monkey, camel, stork, lamb, antelope, giraffe, fawn, and elephant; Nosco Plastic, Erie, PA, **set, $20.***

*Campus Cuties, Louis Marx Co., Inc., 1964; each is about 6" tall, **each, rare, $25.***

*Sinclair dinosaurs sold at the New York World's Fair, 1964–1965, for 25¢ each; you could put your money in a machine and actually watch them being made. Some are marked Dino or Dinoland; 5"–7" long; each; **$10.***

Marbleized

Very recently, interest in marbleized toys—those with the mottled look—has taken hold. Several are pictured in this chapter. Prices on these toys, which are still low, are likely to rise, so don't ignore them.

*Red and yellow plastic dogsled with rubber dog, 5" long, **$15;** marbleized gray and red cruise ship, 4" long, **$10;** and Tiny Tools on original card (including marbleized pink or green saw, rake, hammer, and shovel), Lido Toy Corp., NYC, **$20.***

*Horse nodder, brown with white stockings, 2" high, **$28.** Marbleized donkey, 1½" high, **$22.***

Nodders

Nodders, now called *bobbin' heads* by most collectors, are not new to the market: You can find beautiful bisque ones from the nineteenth century, for instance. By contrast, collectible plastic nodders were made in the 1950s and 1960s, so the trend toward collecting them is fairly recent, yet some of their prices are already high. Basically, though, if you are willing to invest $10–$35, you can acquire a respectable collection of these plastic toys.

Poodle nodder, black, S. A. Reider and Co., Germany, 2" high, $25. Camel nodder/walker, brown, $22.

Nodders' heads, and sometimes tails, mouths, and ears, move by various means. Some bounce on a wire spring, while others rock on small plastic prongs. Still others jiggle back and forth or side to side on a variety of ingenious attachments. Some dog nodders have heads that make a nearly 360-degree rotation while their mouths comically open and close.

Among the most popular nodders are the small ones, 3 inches high (or less), especially those made by S. A. Reider of Germany. Notice the little goose at the top of page 152.

Pez Candy Containers

Pez candy containers are already in great demand, and prices are on the rise. Even so, a collection can still be amassed cheaply enough by scouring flea markets and yard sales. Many of the containers can still be bought for five cents each at a yard sale.

Availability. Since the 1960s, collectors have been finding Pez containers in dime stores, discount department stores, and drugstores. If you're about to start a collection, you might want to see what is being made right now so you don't pay too much at a show for one that's still in production.

As crossover collectibles, certain Pez containers will become increasingly scarce. Holiday collectors will be competing for Easter, Christmas, and the most recently escalating fad, Halloween containers. Many who collect antique glass candy containers have silently started adding Pez to their collections. Toy collections will feature some of the better containers, and even subject collections (particularly animal ones) will contain one or two.

Parts. Pez containers can be listed by the number of parts in each. To count the parts, add the number of separate pieces on the head or section that ejects the candy to the number 2 (which accounts for the head itself and the handle). For example, Mickey Mouse has a separate nose, for a total of 3 parts. Scrooge McDuck has a top hat, sideburns, and spectacles, so he is a Number 5. A Number 6 is the most complicated Pez container I have, but there may be higher numbers. (See Chapter 14 and the color section for Pez container photographs.)

Usually those with more parts are worth more because they cost more to make, there are fewer of them, and the parts tend to get lost.

Country of origin. Try to get similar containers from different countries. I have containers made in the U.S.A., Austria, Yugoslavia, and Hong Kong, but have not seen any made in Japan.

In terms of price, the character and company mark on the Pez containers (see Chapter 14) are usually more important to collectors than the country of origin.

Walkers

Like nodders, plastic walkers are of fairly recent interest to collectors. Some of the first were made in the late 1940s, and they were well received throughout the 1960s and 1970s.

One type of walker has feet that move when the toy is set on an incline. These walkers are usually comical, and many depict Disney characters. Pictured here are a group of walkers which fit in the first group. (See Chapter 1 for a close-up of the pair of soldiers.)

Flintstones, $75. Soldiers, $20. Donald Duck with wheelbarrow, early 1950s, $30. Minnie Mouse with baby buggy, $30. Mickey Mouse with roller, 1946–1947, $35.

Dachshund walker, brown, $20. Black and white cat walker (with eight feet), $35.

Another type of walker was weighted. (Often the plastic weight is now missing, but usually a tiny loop remains at the front of the toy.) A string was tied to this loop, and the walker was then placed near the end of a table. As the weight was dropped over the edge of the table, it pulled the toy along, making it "walk."

Dog (which moves when plunger is pushed at opposite end of wire) with cardboard doghouse marked Champ Junior, J. P. Gowland, Revell Toys—Play Planned, Controlit Toys, *$30.*

Expect cartoon character walkers to be the most expensive, usually $35 and up.

Condition

Toy condition affects pricing to a major degree. In most cases, the more recent the toy, the more important that it be MIB (Mint—In Box).

Cracks, scratches, and missing or broken parts all detract from the toy's value. Use the following guidelines to help you determine what to pay for toys in varying conditions until you become comfortable making the estimates yourself.

- *MIB.* Increases the toy's value by 50 percent.
- *Cracks* or *missing parts.* Decrease value by 50–75 percent.
- *Severe scratches.* Decrease value by 30 percent.
- *Minor scratches.* Decrease value by 10 percent.

Remember, these are just guidelines. Collectors must decide for themselves how much to raise or lower the market value of a toy based on its condition.

Green Jeryco stroller with removable doll, original box, 1940s, $20.

Banner Fountainette, child's fountain set, Plastics Corp., MIB, $45.

Cannon key-ring puzzle, 2" long, $10. Red and white canoe with oar, $15.

Red, yellow, blue, green, and pink motorcycle, 5" long, $18, and red, blue, and yellow steam shovel, 2" high, $20.

Mechanical toy car made to resemble a tiger— the mouth moves, $25.

Good Prospects

While the range of manufacturing dates on these toys spans 100 years—from early Celluloids to the recent Star Wars toys— surprisingly, some of the more recent ones sell for more than those remaining from the nineteenth century. Take a look at the high prices some toys are already bringing, and then take advantage of the fact that great buys remain available almost everywhere because not everyone is familiar with the current market.

In your collecting, look for the following company names:

Acme	Maco
Amsco	Manoil
Archer	Marx
Bachman	Mattel
Banner	Mego
Benton	Nosco Plastic
Dakin	Plastic Art
Gilmark	Pressman
Gund	Pyro
Hartland	Rembo
Hubley	Renwal
Ideal	Revell
Irwin	Saunders
Kaymar	S. A. Reider (Germany)
Kenner	Thomas Dam
Lido	Wannatoys

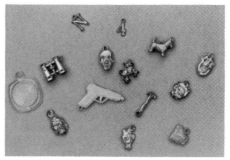

Charms from the penny gumball machines, $2-$12. (The higher prices go for popular characters such as Dopey, pictured at lower right.)

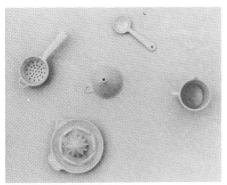

Red baseball bank with white bats, **$35.**

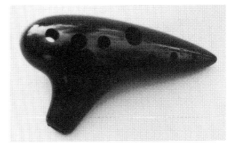

Bakelite ocarina (flutelike instrument commonly called a sweet potato by musicians today), **$18.**

Amsco toy dishes, yellow, **each, $2–$3.** (Irwin children's dishes are in the same price range.)

"The Bunny Easter Party," child's picture disk, **$10.**

Assortment of toy food, very lightweight, 1950s–1960s, **set, $18.**

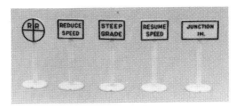

Signs for an electric train yard, white with painted black lettering, 1950s, **set of 5, $22.**

19

Jewelry Items

During the mid-1800s, ivory was so widely used for articles such as jewelry that game-preservation laws were passed in Africa to end the killing of elephants. In fact, John W. Hyatt's first experiments with Celluloid, which lead to his 1870 patent for the substance, were prompted by a contest—held by a billiard ball company—offering $10,000 for a substitute for ivory. With this barrier broken, jewelry manufacturers began to produce a wide range of Celluloid items which were carefully crafted as imitation ivory, right down to the tiny, evenly spaced striations.

Celluloid also took the form of imitation tortoiseshell. Bakelite and other plastics were made to copy other natural, more expensive materials—jade, malachite, marble, jet, onyx, lapis, and mother-of-pearl. These copies were even faceted like real gemstones or made into beads. In addition, real gems and pearls were sometimes set into plastics, or plastics were mounted on precious metals such as silver and gold.

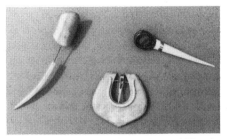

Pearlized pink Celluloid stickpin, $30. Art Deco belt buckle, pearlized Celluloid with rhinestones, 1930s, $30. White "tooth" stickpin, $25.

Bakelite rings: (top) green and black dome, $50; (center) carved red, $68, orange dome, $35, smooth red, $35; (bottom) green dome, $42.

Ball stickpin in butterscotch Catalin and sterling silver, $45. Celluloid girl pin, painted decoration, $68.

Butterscotch Catalin bangle bracelet with rhinestone decoration, 2¹/₂″ wide, $140. Hand-carved collar pin in cream-colored Celluloid, $38.

non, soon even Coco Chanel was adding a piece of plastic jewelry here and there at fashion shows, with Art Deco design as the focal point. Today, Bakelite and Celluloid jewelry continue to find favor as collectibles, with signed pieces (such as those from French designer August Bonaz) commanding very interesting prices.

Assorted Pins

Top row:
*Green Bakelite cherries pin, **$85**, and blue Bakelite bouquet with rhinestones and black leaves, **$40**.*

Middle row:
*Layered Celluloid cardinal (red), **$38**; spangled acrylic arrow pin, **$35**, spangled acrylic parrot pin, **$28**, and Celluloid cornucopia, **$29**.*

Bottom row:
*Tortoiseshell (Celluloid) arrow bar pin with rhinestones, **$30**.*

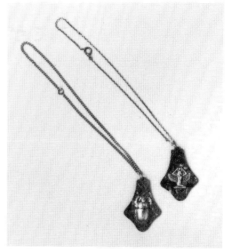

*Art Deco necklaces: red, black, and yellow marbleized Bakelite; 1930s. One has a scarab metal mount; the other mount is also Egyptian. **Each, $145**.*

George F. Berkander was one of the first Americans to imagine that Celluloid jewelry could be beautiful. In the 1920s, he began to manufacture a conservative line of plastic jewelry (in the style of the time). At first there were skeptics, but eventually even major New York department stores bought his wares. Other companies soon followed suit, and millions of Celluloid jewelry items were turned out every day in the 1930s.

Because Bakelite is basically more massive than Celluloid, it could be used to make more substantial jewelry, and it became popular as well. Although the sophisticated fashion community attempted to ignore this preoccupation with plastics as a middle-class phenome-

Counterclockwise: *translucent red acrylic bow-tie pin, **$48**; pearlized gray Art Deco belt buckle with black accents, **$30**; butterscotch Bakelite Art Deco buckle squares with chocolate ball decoration, **$30**; translucent green and blue-green acrylic tear-drop pin, **$40**.*

Amber Bakelite necklace with Art Deco-style drops on metal mounts, $95. Amber Bakelite pin, also in the Deco style, $80.

Bakelite figural pins (clockwise): brown and black swan and vaseline swordfish, both hand-carved, each, $95–$125; dog (he holds his leash in his mouth), $100–$135; butterscotch horse head (rare because of the added tack), $95–$125.

Necklace, black Bakelite cubes alternating with red balls, $180.

Pins (top to bottom): Carved black, $60. Black and mother-of-pearl, $95. Black with spots, $75.

Production and Design Factors

Some pieces of Bakelite jewelry were made from sheets, rods, tubes, or slabs of material. Carved pins and clips were first stamped from sheets or thick slabs, then carved with semiautomatic jigsaws and lathes, and polished in a machine much like a rock tumbler. Deeply carved pieces required additional hand-polishing methods.

The more intricate and carefully finished the handwork, the more desirable the jewelry. Inspect carved items for unpolished areas in deep crevices. Rough places indicate hand carving that was not completely polished.

Assorted Bakelite

Top row:
Button earrings, **pair,** *$15; cherries-on-a-log pin, $95; carved red dress clip, $20.*

Middle row:
Brown acorn dress clips, **pair,** *$25; carved circle pin (green), $40; palm tree pin, $95; Dutch shoe novelties,* **pair,** *$39; carved green Bakelite mounted in metal,* **pin and earrings,** *$60.*

Bottom row:
Carved leaf dress clip (black), $14; carved ivory dress clip, $18; black bar pin, $30; ivory arrow pin, $29.

A pair of hand-carved "V for Victory" Bakelite pins; one is solid brown; the other, red, $20.

Dotted Bakelite rings, **each, $140,** *and earrings,* **pair, $145.**

Bakelite pieces cast in molds do not have the deep carving shown on hand-finished items. Dated pieces with Bakelite rods sliced and embedded in the cast, however, are expensive and rare.

Other pieces were made by injection molding (defined in Chapter 2). These are not as sturdy as the carved pieces.

In particular, bracelets are expensive collectibles today and were expensive even when they were first produced because of the handwork their production required. They were cut from tubes and then subjected to the same carving and polishing techniques described above.

Injection molded Bakelite bracelet, **$180–$250.** *Dotted Bakelite bracelets,* **each, $180–$200.**

*Butterscotch, red, and green Bakelite stretch-link bracelets, **each, $65.***

*Earrings: red Bakelite balls, **pair, $45;** black circles and glitter embedded in acrylic, **pair, $28;** lime Bakelite embedded in metal, **pair, $30.***

*Cuff bracelet, black Bakelite, **$200.** Heart buckle, brown Bakelite, **$60.***

Similarly, some pins were sliced from rods molded into a shape such as a leaf, so when the rod was sliced, the perimeter of the object already had the desired shape, and carving and details were all that were necessary.

Reverse carving. A reverse-carved piece has a design carved into the back of it. Normally, hand-colored, transparent resin (without the filler used to give it the opaque effect) was used for such a piece.

Details. Finishing touches on Bakelite jewelry included rhinestones, pearls or faux pearls, leather, fabric, chains, beads, strings holding attachments, and even a real gem or two (an item from the latter group is a rare find). In some cases, clasps were added, and sometimes rivets were used for attachments. Finally, look for inlay and for lamination, in which several layers of Bakelite laminated together create a striped effect around the edges of the piece.

Bakelite pins (counterclockwise): *ivory fawn with real leather ears, **$90;** orange Scottie bar pin, **$65;** yellow elephant and red Scottie, **each, $45;** acrylic fish with green eye, **$60.***

*Lime green and butterscotch Bakelite stacked bracelet with dice motif, **$200.***

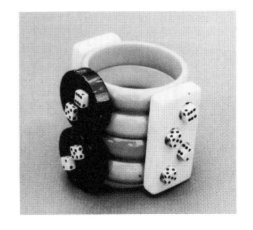

Black, yellow, and red striped bracelet, 1960s, **$50.** Also pictured: *Red scarf ring with rhinestones,* **$30.**

Bracelets. Bracelets have several design peculiarities. *Cuffs* fit (*clip*) over the arm in a C shape. Some bracelets are hinged circles that wrap completely around the arm, and some are expandable (strung on elastic); the latter type can be restrung if it breaks. Then there are bangles, shaped like unbroken circles, which were often worn several at a time. Look for them in wide, brightly colored bands.

Dating by Style and Composition

Collectibles from the 1920s are rather delicate pieces made from Celluloid, Galalith (a casein-based product), and Bakelite.

From the 1920s and 1930s, look for the Art Deco styling features and motifs mentioned in Chapter 3: chrome accents; whippets; flappers; Egyptian influence; Aztec, Mayan, or other Indian influences; Cubism and geometric design; speed lines; speedy objects like airplanes and automobiles; and streamlining.

From the 1940s look for whimsical designs: large Bakelite hearts, bowling pins, animal shapes, and lots of food—cherries, grapes, bananas, and so on. *Big, beautiful, bizarre,* and *brash* were the key adjectives for plastic jewelry from this period.

Catalin pins: yellow ladybug on hand-carved leaf, **$110;** *emerald green owl (with applied acrylic eyes) peering out from a tree fork,* **$95;** *squirrel perched on log,* **$95.** *Art Deco horsehead pin in marbleized green, yellow, and black,* **$125.**

Necklace with dangling oranges and Celluloid chain, **$325.** **Rare.**

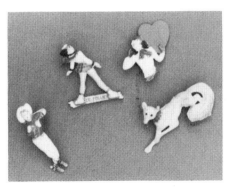

Cherry Bakelite bracelet (red), **$180,** *and earrings,* **pair, $65.**

Cowboy ring, 1940s, **$25.** *Ice Follies skater, cream with red and black accents, 1950s,* **$35.** *"Hubba Hubba" pin,* **$25.** *Celluloid fox pin,* **$40.**

The 1950s popularized poodles and records and the rock-and-roll age of Elvis Presley. Bakelite retreated into the background in favor of more modern hard plastics.

With the 1960s, plastic jewelry sported geometric designs, stylized flowers, and translucent rings. Beads were a favorite, and again, music memorabilia (Beatles items, pins, and plenty of guitars) took the form of plastic jewelry.

Keep in mind that these periods do overlap on occasion, and that material, style, design, and manufacturing techniques all contribute to determining the age of an item.

The Current Market

Prices on certain kinds of plastic jewelry have already skyrocketed, especially for choice Bakelite pieces, but most non-collectors don't realize its value yet, so you can find some good buys.

Assorted Bakelite rings made in West Virginia State Prison between 1932 and 1937, **each, $100–$150.**

Red and black Bakelite ring holders, **each, $48. Rare.** *(Celluloid ring, $22.)*

The best place to buy Bakelite jewelry are flea markets and antiques shops specializing in Art Deco and contemporary collectibles. Antique jewelry shops may also carry it, depending on the interests of the dealer.

Keep in mind that many dealers will be alert for special items for you—if you get to know them and become a good customer. The best objects, in all types of antique circles, are often held back for "special" customers.

Miniature black shoes dangling from Celluloid link chain, $140. Black bow-tie bar pin, $165.

Silver-plated pin with pencil and erasable note-pad (each leaf of the pad is marked for a day of the week), $95. Silver-plated cover with fold-out comb, $28.

Currently, dots, uncommon figures, bunch pins (those with dangling strings of objects), fruit necklaces, and laminated objects are bringing high prices. On the other hand, dress clips, plain bangles, plain earrings, and small pieces are not popular right now.

Good Prospects

Plastic jewelry is now drawing the attention given to jewelry made with gems and precious metals. Some collectors are actually selling real gems to buy Bakelite. As the demand for such jewelry heightens, it is sure to win the place it deserves among antiques and collectibles, and more publi-

cations will address this collecting trend with something other than a casual mention.

Bracelets

Acrylic bracelet with enameled metal mounts in assorted colors, **$18.**

Art Deco acrylic bracelet, 1930s–1940s, **$45.**

Link bracelets:
a. Brown Bakelite, **$65.**
b. Large-link, brown Bakelite, **$60.**
c. Pearlized yellow, **$45.**
d. Red Bakelite, **$80.**

Pins and Charms

Acrylic horse, cranberry, **$40.**

Back-carved acrylic pin with black-eyed susan, **$45.**

Bakelite ball pin with large rhinestone, green, **$40.**

Bakelite flute bar pin, black, **$70.**

Bakelite heart with kissing German figures, **$95.**

Bakelite sword with chain, green, **$68.**

Bar pin with wooden center and red Bakelite ends, **$50.**

Black sword pin with diamond rhinestones, **$50.**

Carved Bakelite collar pins, green flowers, **$40**, ivory, **$42.**

Carved Bakelite conch shell, ivory, **$85.**

Carved Bakelite horse head with acrylic mane, green, **$110.**

Carved Bakelite rose, red, **$85.**

Carved Bakelite sword, salmon, **$35.**

Circular Lucite pin with carved red and white Bakelite center, **$60.**

Avon pins: Calico cat, 1974–1975, $6; Fly-A-Kite, 1983, $5; Sniffy Pin Pal (black skunk), $10; Chick-A-Peek perfume egg, $9.

Pins: palm trees, $45; pastel basket of flowers, $32; white Scottie (with initials), $30; rope, $15.

Bakelite heart pins, red on black and ivory on red, each, $180.

Red acorn bar pin with gold-color metal mount, **$60.**

Red heart with painted *Be My Valentine,* **$40.**

Assorted

Celluloid necklace box (cream), fabric-lined, marked *Deltalt,* Brown-Crystal Manufacturing Company, **$30.**

Dark green Bakelite necklace in the Art Deco style, **$65,** and matching bracelet, **$45.** (The chains are Celluloid.) Black hand-carved Bakelite bow, **$125.** All 1930s.

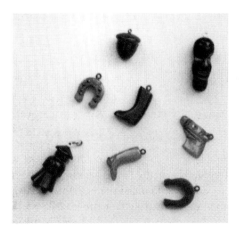

*Bakelite charms; carved black and red African mask, butterscotch horse head, maroon horseshoe, red acorn, brown boot, butterscotch boot and horseshoe, black Oriental figure, **each** $25–$35.*

169

Engraved acrylic jewelry box with embedded golden strips (called spangles*), $50.*

Red and black Bakelite display stands **(rare)**.

Back row:
a. *Small,* **$125.**
b. *Medium,* **$175.**
c. *Large, $225.*
Front row:
d. *Double stand, $125.*
e./f. *Card stands,* **each, $150.**

Ring box, turquoise-colored, Dennison, USA, **$15.**

Jewelry store display boxes, cream and orange Bakelite with velvet liners: single ring box, $90; double, $95; bracelet, $225. **Rare.**

Acrylic ring holders with burgundy velvet liners, **each, $30.**

Speidel watch box with shell-shaped feet, cream, $25.

Dress clips, green Bakelite with metal beading, **$30,** ivory with Art Deco circles, **$22.**

20

Miscellaneous Fashion Items

Attractive plastic fashion articles have been popular throughout the twentieth century, for both their economy and durability. As with so many other plastic collectibles, they originally flourished as copies of products made from scarcer materials, but today have themselves become desirable.

Chignon barrette, imitation tortoiseshell, $28.

Counterclockwise (from top):
a. *Imitation tortoiseshell comb (needs pin),* **$40** *(if complete).*
b. *White comb with rhinestones,* **$20.**
c. *Tortoiseshell (Celluloid) comb with amethyst-colored rhinestones,* **$75.**
d. *Imitation tortoiseshell comb, pierced,* **$45.**
e. *Imitation tortoiseshell comb, plain,* **$20.**
f. *Butterscotch Celluloid comb with rhinestones, c1900,* **$10.**
Center: *Imitation tortoiseshell comb with rhinestones, c1900–1915,* **$40.**

Tortoiseshell (Celluloid) comb with cobalt blue rhinestones, **$80.**

Celluloid fan, **$30.**

171

Celluloid fan with each segment cut out and fashioned by hand, just like real tortoiseshell; the original tassel is purple, $68.

Buttons

Before the advent of man-made plastics, buttons were made of natural materials: mother-of-pearl, ivory, bone, horn, and leather. Then came the introduction of Celluloid. Among these early plastic buttons, the ones made to imitate ivory are known to collectors as *ivoroids*.

Casein has been used in buttons since it was first manufactured in 1913 in England, where it was called *Emeloid*. Note that some early buttons are marked *casein* on the back.

In the 1930s, wartime shortages of raw materials caused manufacturers to opt for Bakelite instead of the more expensive casein and Celluloid. Also in wartime, plastic buttons were first electroplated to resemble metal, a process which continued long after the war.

Buttons made of other new plastic materials had different problems early on. For example, polystyrene buttons turned yellow from exposure to sun, so chemists added suntan lotion to their basic formula.

Bakelite. By the 1930s, then, Bakelite had become the preferred material for buttons. Because Bakelite could be carved, buttons made from it appeared in a wide range of shapes. From this group, large Art Deco buttons, usually with geometric designs, are quite collectible today, and several are pictured in this chapter.

Realistics. The late 1940s saw the birth of realistics, or novelty buttons that resembled real objects such as boats, birds, people, toys, flowers, and fruits and vegetables (part of the recurring Carmen Miranda influence). "School Days" buttons (c1930), for instance, resemble blackboards.

*Assorted buttons (realistics): Bakelite, **each, $15;** Lucite, **each, $10;** other plastics, **each $6.***

Value. Some of these buttons have become very rare and are quite expensive today. The buttons pictured in this chapter are small shapes; the higher-priced varieties are more like the charms in the jewelry chapter.

Plastic Disney buttons from the 1930s and 1940s, which are very rare, also bring high prices. The best can sell for $30 or more, depending on novelty and rarity.

Other considerations. Although they're still relatively new, don't overlook the flamboyant 1960s buttons and modern plastic realistics; even today, there are still plenty of interesting buttons being manufactured. Examine flea market and yard sale clothing for good buys. Checking old coats is another good way to find Bakelite buttons.

Spangled acrylic umbrella handle, $20.

Other Items

A number of other fashion items are becoming plastic collectibles. Exceptional Celluloid (and other types of plastic) cane tops should fare well in collecting circles. Celluloid fans, imitations of the more expensive ivory and tortoiseshell versions, also appeal to collectors. Eyeglasses—the 1950s rhinestone-studded plastics as well as the oversized 1960s versions—are attracting interest, and teddy bear collectors are adorning their finds with early eyeglasses to give them a distinguished air.

Sunglasses, 1950s and 1960s, **pair, $8–$18.**

Hand-carved Bakelite claw clutching a ball (designed to hang on a chain), $175–$250. Hand-carved Bakelite dog cane top, $125–$165.

Black Celluloid spectacles, $30.

Unique plastic purses are in demand, as well. In particular, 1940s purses with fair prices and handsome, pearlized exteriors rarely stay with a dealer very long. If you see one of these purses for less than $20, buy it; also look for those with designer labels.

Ball-and-claw Celluloid-handled cane with silver-plated band and wooden shaft, early 1900s, $75. From the collection of Bud Leister, Westminster, MD.

Pearlized-gold-colored purse with back-carved acrylic lid and pearlized brown acrylic trim, **$75.**

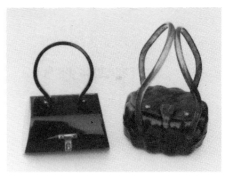

Black acrylic purse, **$45.** Tortoiseshell-colored purse, **$42.**

Lozenge-shaped purse, caramel acrylic with clear acrylic sides, **$50.**

Translucent acrylic purse with reddish, striped highlights, **$38.**

Presently, buckles seem to be on the lower end of the collecting scale in terms of value. This might be a good area, however, for the person who collects purely because of personal interest.

*Deer belt buckle, Art Deco, painted gray Celluloid with chrome clasp, 1930s, **$40**.*

*Lime green, back-carved, circle buckle on original card, **$20**.*

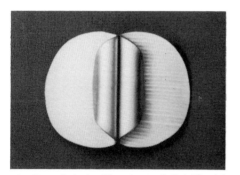

*Art Deco belt buckle, cream Celluloid with painted silver curls, 1930s, **$28**.*

Good Prospects

Any object that makes a fashion statement for a particular era can become collectible. Watch for unique items such as those 1960s wrap-around sunglasses which had a mere slit to see through, or the transparent vinyl women's shoes worn during the last few years.

175

21
Novelties, Souvenirs, and Holiday-Related Collectibles

Actually, the entire price guide is devoted to novelties, but the ones included in this chapter are novelties in the sense that they are knickknacks which basically serve no other purpose than to provide some decorative interest. Similarly, you will find souvenirs scattered throughout this book, since all types of objects were emblazoned with place names and sold to visitors as keepsakes. Again, those featured in this chapter were intended basically for ornamental value.

Vinyl "I'm Sorry!" statue, Dakin, 8" high, **$10.**

Plastic pink flamingo and mermaid set in plaster, Lily Tulip Cup Corp., NY, **$35.**

Canadian Mountie, painted red, marked Reliable, *Canada, 7½" high,* **$15.**

Pale green, leaf-shaped candy dish with flamingo painted in the center, marked Silver Springs, Fla., **$10.** *Also pictured:* Green Bakelite salt and pepper shakers with glass dome tops, Art Deco, 1930s, **pair, $20.**

The final, closely related category covered here is holiday-related collectibles. Although many of these are Christmas items, a few other types are pictured.

Plastic Easter baskets in solid green or yellow, 1940s, **each, $8.**

Easter Express wagon; bright pink, yellow, and green; 7" × 8"; **$30. Rare.**

Pink, blue, and red Easter rabbits, 3" high, **each, $12.** *Rabbit pull toy, 6" high,* **$30 (rare).** *Yellow rabbit candy container,* **$10.**

Green witch flashlight for trick-or-treating at night, 1960, $30. **Rare.**

Halloween Zooks, 5½" high, **each, $28.** *Witch candy container with hollow pumpkin for holding treats, 4" high, $20.*

Happy Birthday cake wheel (it moves when the switch is flipped) with paper decoration, original box, Sales Development Corp., Atlanta, GA, $20.

Hard-to-find candy container: Valentine's Day girl holding a heart, white with red trim, 3½" high, $20. Heart-shaped candy box, 2½" × 1", $10.

Novelties

Celluloid novelties are highly collectible today, often commanding prices above $20 if they are fairly complex. Hand-carved Celluloid and Bakelite objects are also bringing good prices.

Many collectible novelties are plastic figures—people or animals. Notice the rickshaw, below.

Black and white Celluloid Scottie magnets, ¾", **pair, $20.** *Celluloid dog wearing a top hat, hand-carved Celluloid and Bakelite, $35. Hand-carved Scottie in a top hat, 2½" high, $45.*

Rickshaw, assorted colors, probably made after WWII, 8½" long, $30.

179

Chimney sweep (probably urea), $20. Accordion player, $18.

Red and black salt and pepper shaker set: Plastic red umbrella shakers hang from a hat rack; common, $18. Celluloid kittens riding on a 3″ × 1¾″ sliding board; black, cream, and red; 1930s, $35. Bakelite cat figure, $30.

Black Art Deco box (top), $75. Black and red box, 1930s, $95.

Pink Celluloid religious statue with metal central medallion, Art Deco style, marked CDF, Milano, 1930s, $25.

Red box with white flower, $10.

*Bakelite Art Deco top hat, **$225**. **Rare**. Open view shows spaces for four bottles of perfume.*

*Boy Scout napkin ring, 1920s, **$140**. **Rare**.*

*Large cubes made to resemble dice, Bakelite, red or white, 3" high, **pair, $65**.*

*A New York designer created these contemporary novelties by gluing together Bakelite cubes: black and white candleholders, **pair, $50**, and red and white cigarette box, **$35**.*

Souvenirs

Since Celluloid was cheap, it was often used to manufacture the souvenirs which are now collectible. As you look for them, remember that objects do not have to be marked with the name of a place or event, but need only represent it in some way, in order to be considered souvenirs.

A special item in this category is the plastic snow ball (or snow dome) issued by thousands of tourist attractions and historical sites, many of which are marked *HK* (Hong Kong). Most sell for $5–$35, but higher prices are paid for the rare ones. For instance, domes from lesser-known tourist attractions, military-related domes, and those that advertise businesses are priced higher, selling for $20 and up. Christmas ones are the most common and the least desirable, except for Santa shapes.

*New York World's Fair butter dish (with original box), silver-tone plastic with a transparent base, Miss Fair Gifts, Inc., Long Island, NY, 1964–1965, **$12**.*

181

New York World's Fair snow ball (snow dome); orange, blue, and clear plastic filled with water and "snow," 1964–1965, $25.

Souvenirs from the 1939 World's Fair: butterscotch, orange, and black pencil sharpener (at left), $45; red and black thermometer, $45.

New York World's Fair coasters, silver-tone plastic inserts on solid black circles, 1964–1965, set of 4, $10.

Bakelite thermometer key marked SALISBURY BEACH, MASS., *$15.*

Red Celluloid piano (the top opens to create a cache box), marked INDIAN LAKE, *2" × 1³/₄", Japan, $45.*

Green candleholders with red accents (probably urea), USA, 1930s, 4" high, **pair, $20.**

Celluloid animals such as were usually seen in Christmas tree yards: bulldog, 3⅝" long, **$15–$25,** *and horse with separately attached ears, 4½" long,* **$25.**

Celluloid camel, 3½" long, **$23.** *Celluloid elephant, 4" long,* **$25.**

Unusual bowling trophy made with metal mounts on black, cream, and marbleized burgundy Bakelite, **$20.** *Not pictured: Celluloid bowling lighter, 2" high,* **$35.**

Holiday-Related Collectibles

Many collectors have become infatuated with holiday-related collectibles, perhaps because of the good times and childhood memories they represent. Whatever the reason, the value of some of these is rapidly increasing, so if you want to collect them, start now. You might still be able to find some good buys for a dollar or two.

White church, green house, and white house (also for Christmas yard) with indentation on base for light bulb, 1940s, **each, $10.** *Not pictured: Evergreen tree (flat) with glitter decoration, 5⅛" high,* **$5.**

White choirboys, 3½" tall, **each, $5**, flank a white angel with gold accents, 4" tall, **$9**.

Christmas light-bulb covers, 2" high, made of old plastic, probably urea: yellow cat, **$20**; red dog, **$20**; white angel, **$18**; and Santa, **$22**. Not pictured: snowman, **$18**, and yellow rabbit, **$15**. (Prices are for covers in good condition. Most of these I see have deteriorated from the heat of the Christmas tree bulb put inside.)

Blue, bullet-shaped nativity set in original box, Hong Kong, **$9**.

Christmas collectibles are by far the most popular, with the highest demand being for Santa Claus items and Celluloid animals for the yard. Prices on candy containers and other hard plastics are rising, but for older marbleized objects, which are hard to find because there are so many buyers for them, prices nevertheless remain low in some areas.

Original green and red bubble lights filled with amber or red liquid, **each, $7**. Not pictured: Bubble light candlesticks, **pair, $125**.

Plastic Santa with real rabbit-fur beard and belt, **$32**. Santa with white sleigh candy container, **$25**. Not pictured: Santa and multicolored sleigh candy container, **$18**.

Consider the objects in this field which are marked *Japan* and *Hong Kong*; many have been around for a long time. Also look for brand names, like Kaymar and Knickerbocker, which may add value.

Christmas tree reindeer, available in either beige or white, 1950s; 3¼" high, 3" long. **Each, $15.**

Santa Claus, Kaymar, 5½" tall, **$25.**

Santa Claus doll wearing a rare gold coat, white velour trousers, and hard plastic boots, 13¾" tall, **$80.**

Santa riding a toy Christmas tree car, Hong Kong, **$18.** Not pictured: *Santa on skis, common, 3" × 4½",* **$20.**

Four snow-white reindeer pulling a red, flocked sleigh full of Christmas greenery, $20.

Mr. and Mrs. Santa Claus riding in a golden airplane decorated with a tinsel propeller, $30. **Rare.**

Vinyl Santa with cotton beard, Hong Kong, 7³/₄" tall, $25.

Mechanical house bank: Santa pops out of the chimney when the money is inserted into the slot in the roof; Fun World, Hong Kong, $20. Santa pops out of the chimney of the other bank when the lid is lifted; Hong Kong, $12.

Celluloid Santa nodder (in excellent condition), $325.

Vinyl wind-up Santa with original box, Alps, Japan, $40.

Good Prospects

Of the three categories listed in this chapter, it seems easiest to predict which souvenirs will be especially collectible in the future. Olympics-related objects, or plastics relating to the one-hundredth anniversary of the Statue of Liberty, for example, should become significant, so keep a close watch on such potential collectibles as these.

Wind-up, happy-faced Santa (the top half moves when he is wound), 6" high, $35. Not pictured: *Santa walker, $38.*

APPENDICES

Reindeer (also with loops for hanging them on the Christmas tree), 1940s, **each, $15.**

A

Care and Cleaning Tips

Once you've found an item you're pleased with, you want to be sure to keep it in good condition. Some of the descriptions in Chapter 2 caution you about problems with particular plastics; here is some more specific information about cleaning and caring for your collectibles.

Cleaning and Polishing

One of the main things to remember about plastic is that it scratches easily, so you should never use abrasive cleaners or scouring pads to clean it. Most plastics can be wiped down with a warm, soapy cloth and dried with a soft cloth. To reach small areas, use a toothbrush or cotton swab.

Modern hard plastics are made to withstand hot, soapy water. Industrial-strength hand cleaner may remove ink from these plastics and from some vinyls. But *always* check a small area before you try something like this. It's good to save some odd pieces to experiment on, too.

Bakelite and some early plastics may respond well to aerosol polishes. A friend of mine secretly uses bathroom-cleaning spray foam on her Bakelite radios.

Metal polish or car wax and rubbing compound will often take off surface scratches from some types of plastic, but again, be sure to do a test area first. Also, try the polish used to take scratches out of airplane windshields. (Just call your local airport to ask about the polish—even my small town sells it.)

Adhesive-backed tags should never be used on plastic, since the adhesives might damage the surface. If this kind of tag was already on the object when you bought it, try Andrea DiNoto's suggestion from *Art Plastic*: Use turpentine for removing adhesives. Never use lighter fluid to remove price tags, since lighter fluid will dissolve many types of plastic. Permanent ink markers may also mar surfaces.

Storing and Treating Celluloid

As mentioned in Chapter 2, Celluloid is a special problem because it is flammable and must be kept in a clean, well-ventilated area. Do not expose it to sun or temperatures over 120° F.

In addition, some Celluloid will degenerate. If it has already started to decompose, soak it in washing soda, let it dry, and then coat it with clear nail polish.

B

Trademarks

Bakelite (molded phenolic resin)

Acrolite	Consolidated Molded Products Corp.
Aqualite	National Vulcanized Fiber Co.
Arcolite	Consolidated Molded Products Corp.
Bakelite	Bakelite Corp.
Catabond	Catalin Corp.
Catalin Phenolic	Catalin Corp.
Crystle	Marblette Corp.
Dilecto	Continental-Diamond Fiber Co.
Durez	Durez Plastics
Fiberite	Fiberite Corp.
Formica	Formica Insulation Co.
Gemstone	A. Knoedler Co.
Hersite	Hersite and Chemical Co.
Indur	Reilly Tar & Chemical Co.
Indurite	Indurite Molding Powders Co., UK
Makelot	Makelot Corp.
Marblette	Marblette Corp.
Meillite	Watertown Manufacturing Co.
Micarta	Westinghouse Electric & Manufacturing Co.
Micoid	Watertown Manufacturing Co.
Monolite	Monowatt Electric Corp.
Resinox	Monsanto Chemical Co.
Ryercite	Joseph T. Ryerson & Son
Super-Beckacite	Reichold Chemicals, Inc.
Synthane	Synthane Corp.
Uniplast	Universal Plastics Co.

Casein

Aralac	National Dairy Products Corp.
Ambroid	Japan
Ameroid	American Plastics Corp.
Coronation	George Morrell Corp.
Gala	George Morrell Corp.
Galalith	International Galalith (early)
Galorn	George Morrell Corp.
Karolith	American Plastics Co.
Kasolid	Synthetic Plastics Co.
Kyloid	Kyloid, USA
Maco	Prolamine Products, Inc.
Pearlalith	B. Schwanda & Sons
Protoflex	Glyco Products Co.

Cast Phenolic Resin

Aquapearl	Catalin Corp.
Bakelite Cast Resinoid	Bakelite Corp.
Catalin	Catalin Corp.
Crystle	Marblette Corp.
Gemstone	A. Knoedler Co.
Marblette	Marblette Corp.
Opalon	Monsanto Chemical Co.
Prystal	Catalin Corp.
Textolite	General Electric Co.

Cellulose Acetate

Acele	E. I. Du Pont de Nemours
Acelose	American Cellulose Co.
Acetyloid	Japan
Amer-glo	Celanese Plastics Corp.
Bakelite Cellulose Acetate	Celanese Celluloid Corp.
Celastoid	Celanese Celluloid Corp.
Cellastine	Celanese Celluloid Corp.
Cellulate	National Plastic Products Corp.
Charmour	Celanese Corp.
Clair de Lune	Celanese Celluloid Corp.
Clearsite	Celluplastic Corp.
Enameloid	Gemloid Corp.
Fibestos	Monsanto Chemical Co.
Gemlite	Gemloid Corp.
Lumarith	Celanese Plastics Corp.
Macite	Manufacturers Chemical Corp.
Marolin	Czecho-Peasant Art Co.
Nixonite	Nixon Nitration Works

Parkite	Parkwood Corp.
Parkwood	Parkwood Corp.
Plastacele	E. I. Du Pont de Nemours
Plasticoil	Schab & Frank, Inc.
Plastoflex	Advance Solvents & Chemical Corp.
Rexenite	The Rexenite Co., Inc.
R-V-Lite	Avery Corp.
Safety Samson	Celanese Celluloid Corp.
Sundora	E. I. Du Pont de Nemours
Tec	Tennessee Eastman Corp.
Tenite I	Tennessee Eastman Corp.
Vimlite	Celanese Plastics Corp.
Vitapane	Avery Corp.
Vuepak	Monsanto Chemical Co.
Vu-lite	Monsanto Chemical Co.

Celluloid (cellulose nitrate)

Amer-glo	Celanese Plastics Corp.
Amerith	Celanese Plastics Corp.
Celastic	Celastic Corp.
Celluloid	Celluloid Manufacturing Co. (early)
	Celanese Plastics Corp. (later)
Celluvarno	Sillcocks-Miller Co.
Dumoid	E. I. Du Pont de Nemours
Fabrikoid	E. I. Du Pont de Nemours
Fiberloid	The Fiberloid Corp.
Herculoid	Hercules Powder Corp.
Hykoloid	Celluplastic Corp.
Keratol	Atlas Powder Co.
Lusteroid	Lusteroid Container Co.
Nitron	Monsanto Chemical Co.
Nixonoid	Nixon Nitration Works
Permanite	Parker Pen Co.
Phoenixite	Japan
Protecto	Celluloid Corp.
Proxyl	Lee S. Smith & Son Man.
Pyralin	E. I. Du Pont de Nemours (early pens)
Pyra-Shell	Shoeform Co.
Radite	Shaeffer Pen Co.
Samson	Carpenter Steel Co.
Simco	Sillcocks-Miller Co.
Viscoloid	E. I. Du Pont de Nemours
Xylonite	David Spill Co. (early)
Zaflex	Atlas Powder Co.
Zakaf	Atlas Powder Co.

Melamine (melamine-formaldehyde)

Catalin Melamine	Catalin Corp.
Formica	Formica Insulation Co.
Melantine	Ciba Products Corp.
Melmac	American Cyanamid Co.
Melurac	American Cyanamid Co.
Micarta	Westinghouse Electric & Manufacturing Co.
Plaskon Melamine	Allied Chemical Corp.
Resimene	Monsanto Chemical Co.
Watertown Ware	Watertown Manufacturing Co.

Polyethelene (Polythene)

Alathon	E. I. Du Pont de Nemours
Carlona	Shell Chemicals
Fortiflex	Celanese Corp.
Marlex	Phillips Petroleum
Poly-Ethylene	E. I. Du Pont de Nemours
Polythene	E. I. Du Pont de Nemours

Polystyrene

Amphenol	American Phenolic Corp.
Bendalite	Bend-A-Lite Plastics
BP Polystyrene	BP Chemicals
Burrite	Burroughs Manufacturing Co.
Carex	Monsanto Chemical Co.
Cyrene	Neville Co.
Laolin	Catalin Corp.
Loavar	Catalin Corp.
Lustrex	Catalin Corp.
Lustro-Ware	Columbus Plastic Products
Plax Polystyrene	Plax Corp.
Plexine	Rohm & Haas Co.
Polyfibre	Dow Chemical Co.
Polyflex	Plax Corp.
Polyweld	American Phenolic Corp.
Resoglaz	Advance Solvents & Chemical Co.
Styraloy	Dow Chemical Co.
Styramic	Monsanto Chemical Co.
Styrex	Dow Chemical Co.
Styrite	Dow Chemical Co.
Styrofoam	Dow Chemical Co.
Styron	Dow Chemical Co.
Waterlite	Watertown Manufacturing Co.

Ureas

Bakelite Urea	Union Carbide Corp.
Bandalasta	Brookes and Adams, England
Beatl, Beetle	American Cyanamid (Beetle Products Co., England)
Beetleware	American Cyanamid (Beetle Products Co., England)
Cibanold	Ciba Products Corp.
Daka-ware	Harvey Davies Molding Co.
Durez Urea	Durez Plastics & Chemical Co.
Formica	Formica Insulation Co.
Lamicoid	Mica Insulator Co.
Plaskon	Allied Chemical Corp.
Plastaloid	Smith-Gaines, Inc.
Rauxite	US Industrial Alcohol Co.
Rhonite	Rohm & Haas Co.
Uformite	Resinous Products & Chemical Corp.
Urac	American Cyanamid Co.

Vulcanite (ebonite, hard rubber)

Cohardite	Connecticut Hard Rubber Co.
Endurance	American Hard Rubber Co.
Mercury	American Hard Rubber Co.
Navy	American Hard Rubber Co.
Resiston	American Hard Rubber Co.

Vinyl, PVC

Elasti-glas	S. Buchsbaum Co.
Elvax	E. I. Du Pont de Nemours
Famenol	General Electric Co.
Formvar	Shawinigan Products Corp.
Frostone	President Suspender Co.
Geon	B. F. Goodrich Chemical Co.
Glam	Pantasote Co.
Korogel	B. F. Goodrich Chemical Co.
Korolac	B. F. Goodrich Chemical Co.
Koroseal	B. F. Goodrich Chemical Co.
Krene	Nut Carbon Co.
Lustrex	Foster-Grant Co.
Luxene	Luxene, Inc.
Naugahyde	Uniroyal
Opalon	Monsanto Chemical Co.
Perflex	Visking Corp.
Permalon	Pierce Plastics
Plioflex	B. F. Goodrich Chemical Co.

Plioform	B. F. Goodrich Chemical Co.
Pliolite	B. F. Goodrich Chemical Co.
Re-dolite	L. C. Chase & Co.
Resproid	Respro, Inc.
Saflex	Monsanto Chemical Co.
Tolex	Textileather Corp.
Turex	Textileather Corp.
Ultron	Monsanto Chemical Co.
Veloflex	Firestone Tire & Rubber Co.
Velon	Firestone Tire & Rubber Co.
Versiflex	Carbide & Carbon Chemicals Corp.
Vinal	Pittsburg Plate Glass Co.
Vinylite	Bakelite Corp.
Vinylseal	Bakelite Corp.
Vinylon	Bakelite Corp.
Vitrolac	RCA Records

The Pin Test

Plastics can be hard to identify, especially for the new collector. Consequently, it may be necessary to do a pin test in order to determine exactly what an object is made of.

A Word of Caution

The pin test involves heating a pin and attempting to insert it into an inconspicuous place on a thermoplastic or thermoset in order to see what odor is released. Although this is a common practice, it can damage an object, so *avoid the pin test whenever possible*. It's better to guess about the composition of old plastics—judging by feel, color, style, use, and manufacturer—rather than to risk damage to an item. (If you're photographing an item at a show, the pin test is useless anyway.) After all, a collectible plastic with good quality and a fine design has value whether it is Bakelite or Catalin, casein or urea.

If you decide to try the pin test anyway, observe the following guidelines:

- Do not perform this test on objects that are very thin.
- Practice on some objects that are not of great value—for example, buy some broken or damaged plastics at flea markets or yard sales to try the test on.
- When you heat the pin, keep the flame you're using away from the object you plan to test. Remember, some plastics (like Celluloid) are highly flammable.

- Do not hold the object near your face when you are inserting the pin.
- Insert the pin in an inconspicuous place.

When applied to a thermoplastic, the pin will go in, smoke, or cause the plastic to thread, according to Andrea DiNoto's *Art Plastic*. Consult Table 1 to identify the plastic by the odor emitted during this test.

A pin will not penetrate a thermoset plastic, but the heat from the test will nevertheless cause the plastic to give off an identifying odor.

Ordering a Tester

A hot-point tester, which eliminates some of the tedium of the pin test, can be purchased from the Gemological Institute of America, an educational and scientific institution devoted to gem-related testing, research, and education. Write to the Institute at 1660 Stewart Street, Santa Monica, CA 90404.

Other Tests

A friction test will work with Celluloid, Bakelite, and Catalin: Simply rub a piece of cloth against the object in question and check for the results indicated in Table 1. Another testing alternative for Celluloid and Bakelite is running warm water over the item and checking for the results indicated in Table 1.

Finally, vinyl always has a distinctive smell, and should require no test for identification.

Table 1. Identifying Plastics from Test Results

Plastic	Pin Test Results	Results of Other Tests
Acrylic	fruity smell	
Amber	pine scent	
Bakelite (molded phenolic resin)	pungent smell of phenol (carbolic acid)	same as pin test results
Casein	odor of scalded milk	
Catalin (cast phenolic resin)	carbolic acid smell	same as pin test results
Cellulose Acetate	vinegary smell	
Celluloid (cellulose nitrate)	camphor/moth-ball smell *Note:* This distinguishes it from real ivory, which it often resembles, because real ivory produces a singed-hair odor with the pin test.	same as pin test results
Ebonite	sulfur smell	
Melamine (melamine formaldehyde)	fishy smell	
Polyethylene	odor of burned or scorched wax	
Polystyrene	gas or marigold smell	
Tortoiseshell	singed-hair odor (may be distinguished from ivory by its brown and yellow spots)	
Ureas	formaldehyde smell	

References

Adams, Jane Ford. "Buttons: When Celluloid Was New." *Spinning Wheel*, June 1970, 46.

Alth, Max. *Collecting Old Radios and Crystal Sets*. Des Moines: Wallace-Homestead Book Co., 1977.

Bell, Jeanenne. *Answers to Questions About Old Jewelry, 1840–1950*. Florence, Alabama: Books Americana, 1985.

Bowen, Glen B. *Collectible Fountain Pens*. Glenview, Illinois: Glen Bowen Communications, 1982.

Collier's Encyclopedia. 1983 ed. s.v. "plastics."

Dalzell, Bonnie. "Antiques of the Future: How One Museum Makes Its Choices." *Spinning Wheel*, March/April 1981, 10–12.

Davern, Melva R. *The Collector's Encyclopedia of Salt and Pepper Shakers*. Paducah, Kentucky: Collector Books, 1985.

"Dawn of a New Day: Another Exhibition for World's Fair Buffs." *Joel Sater's Antiques and Auction News*, September 1980.

DiNoto, Andrea. *Art Plastic—Designed for Living*. New York: Abbeville Press, 1984.

———. "Bakelite Envy." *Connoisseur*, July 1985, 60–69.

"Domino Queen Looks for Other Enthusiasts." *Joel Sater's Antiques and Auction News*, October 1978.

DuBois, J. Harry. *Plastics*. New York: Van Nostrand Reinhold Co., 1977.

DuBois, J. Harry, and Frederick W. John. *Plastics*, 5th ed. New York: Van Nostrand, Inc., 1974.

Encyclopedia Americana. International ed. s.v. "plastics."

Encyclopaedia Britannica: Micropedia Ready Reference. 15th ed. s.v. "Baekeland, Leo Heindrick"; "Bakelite"; "Celluloid"; "cellulose acetate"; "chemical compounds"; "chemicals and additives"; "Hyatt, John Wesley"; "Parkes, Alexander."

Epstein, Diana. *Buttons*. Collectors' Blue Books. New York: Walker and Co., 1967.

Fornwalt, Russell J. "The Beatles Story Continues." *American Collector*, August 1983.

———. "Vintage T.V. and Radio Sets." *Joel Sater's Antiques and Auction News*, February 1983.

Gonis, George. "Interview with a Toy Curator." *Cobblestone*, December 1986, 38–41.

Hanley, Tom. "Where TVs Receive the Best Reception." *Collectibles Illustrated*, May/June 1983.

Hency, Robert. "Renwal Furniture." *Rarities*, May/June 1983, 58–61.

Heide, Robert, and John Gilman. *Dream-Store Parade: Popular Culture 1925–1955*. New York: E. P. Dutton, 1979.

Hine, Thomas. *Populuxe*. New York: Alfred A. Knopf, Inc., 1986.

Hopf, Carroll. "Handcrafted Combs." *Spinning Wheel*, July/August 1970, 16–18.

Hughs, Stephen. *Pop Culture Mania.* New York: McGraw-Hill Book Company, 1984.

Jailer, Mildred. "The 1950s Are Coming." *Rarities*, May/June 1983, 13–23.

Jewel, Brian. "Wireless—For the Collector and All Ships at Sea." *The Antiques Journal*, March 1981.

Jordan, Scotia Lynn. "Beatle Mania." *Collectibles Illustrated*, September/October 1983.

Katz, Sylvia. *Plastics: Common Objects, Classic Designs.* New York: Harry N. Adam, Inc., 1984.

Keller, Bob. "What to Collect in the '80s." *Vintage Plastic*, May 1985, 12–14.

Kerfoot, Glenn. "The Fairest Hobby of Them All." *American Collector*, August 1983.

Ketchum, William C., Jr. *The Collector's Guide to American Antiques: Furniture.* Alfred A. Knopf, Inc., 1982.

King, Constance Eileen. "The Search for an Indestructible Substance." *The Collector's History of Dolls.* New York: Bonanza Books, 1977.

Kovel, Ralph and Terry. "Celluloid Bookmarks Are Novel Collectibles." *Collector's News*, 1985.

Lawrence, Cliff. *Fountain Pens: History, Repair, and Current Values.* Dunnedin, Florida: The Pen Fancier's Club, 1985.

———. *Official P.F.C. Pen Guide.* Dunnedin, Florida: The Pen Fancier's Club, 1982.

Lunde, Otto H. "Collecting Old Cribbage Boards." *Spinning Wheel*, March 1970.

Luscomb, Sally C. *The Collector's Encyclopedia of Buttons.* New York: Bonanza Books, 1972.

Mallinak, John D. "The ABCs of Plastics." *The Antique Trader Weekly*, 3 December 1986, 74–81.

Maloney, John F. *Vintage Cameras and Images.* Florence, Alabama: Books Americana, 1981.

McFadden, Sybill. "Character Celluloids: Collectible Dolls of the Future." *Doll News*, Fall 1976, 27–30.

Michael, George. "Gutta Percha Photo Case." *The Auctioneer*, January 1980, 43.

Morse, Sharon. "World's Fairs of the 1930s." *Rarities*, January/February 1983, 55–59.

Murray, William. "Old Radios and TVs." *Rarities.* March/April 1982, 24–29.

"Novelty Antique Radios Command Good Prices." *The Baltimore Sun*, October 1985. *(Reprint from the Chicago Tribune.)*

O'Brien, Richard. *Collecting Toys.* Florence, Alabama: Books Americana, 1985.

Official 1983 Price Guide to Star Trek and Star Wars Collectibles. Orlando: House of Collectibles, Inc., 1983.

Radcliff, Robert R. "Historic Chessmen." *Spinning Wheel*, November 1974, 12–16.

Robinson, Joleen, and Kay Sellers. *Advertising Dolls: Identification and Value Guide.* Paducah, Kentucky: Collector Books, 1980.

"Rock and Roll Collectibles." *Collectors' Showcase Magazine*, October 1983.

Serpa, Geraldine. "Celluloid Jewelry Brightened Fashions of the '20s." *American Collector*, July 1980, 30–31.

Shuart, Harry Wilson. "Papier-Mâché Candy Containers." *Spinning Wheel*, April 1969, 16–17.

"Victorian Paper-Mâché Furniture." *Kovels on Antiques and Collectibles*, January 1986.

Weiman, Marjorie. "Shave and a Haircut, Two Bits." *Antiques World*, December 1981, 70–73.

World Book Encyclopedia. 1976 ed. s.v. "plastics, Lucite."

Index